The Evolutionary Origins of Markets

"An important further step in the unification of diverse approaches into a coherent, consilient social exchange science."

Gerald A. Cory Jr., Author, Former Senior Fellow, San Jose State University, USA

"The current cutting-edge fields of evolutionary and complexity sciences, cognitive, neuro, brain and behavioral sciences, biological analogies, Institutionalism, Socio-Economics, and the different related computational strands, still are often only loosely connected. Those working in these fields will find this book providing a major step forward by integrating our knowledge on the evolution of human sociality, its cognitive, emotive, and behavioral foundations. While the literature in these fields has been exploding, here we have a most welcome integrating transdisciplinary work. Applying these stocks of knowledge to the foundations and evolution of 'markets,' socio-economists and social scientists of all perspectives will find how to make deeper sense of what we have used to call the social and institutional 'embeddedness of markets.' A highly recommended book."

Prof. Wolfram Elsner, University of Bremen, Germany

Our elaborate market exchange system owes its existence not to our calculating brain or insatiable self-centeredness, but rather to our sophisticated and nuanced human sociality and to the inherent rationality built into our emotions. The modern economic system is helped a lot more than hindered by our innate social instincts that support our remarkable capacity for building formal and informal institutions.

The book integrates the growing body of experimental evidence on human nature scattered across a variety of disciplines from experimental economics to social neuroscience into a coherent and original narrative about the extent to which market (or impersonal exchange) relations are reflective of the basic human sociality that was originally adapted to a more tribal existence.

An accessible resource, this book will appeal to students of all areas of economics, including Behavioral Economics and Neuro-Economics, Microeconomics, and Political Economy.

Rojhat Avşar is an associate professor of economics at Columbia College Chicago. His research and teaching interests include social behavior, ethical norms, economic discourse, origin of human institutions, and political economy.

Economics as Social Theory

Series edited by Tony Lawson
University of Cambridge

Social theory is experiencing something of a revival within economics. Critical analyses of the particular nature of the subject matter of social studies and of the types of method, categories, and modes of explanation that can legitimately be endorsed for the scientific study of social objects, are re-emerging. Economists are again addressing such issues as the relationship between agency and structure, between economy and the rest of society, and between the enquirer and the object of enquiry. There is a renewed interest in elaborating basic categories such as causation, competition, culture, discrimination, evolution, money, need, order, organization, power probability, process, rationality, technology, time, truth, uncertainty, value, etc.

The objective for this series is to facilitate this revival further. In contemporary economics the label "theory" has been appropriated by a group that confines itself to largely asocial, ahistorical, mathematical "modeling." Economics as social theory thus reclaims the "Theory" label, offering a platform for alternative rigorous, but broader and more critical conceptions of theorizing.

48. Keynes Against Capitalism
His Economic Case for Liberal Socialism
James Crotty

49. The Nature of Social Reality
Issues in Social Ontology
Tony Lawson

50. The Evolutionary Origins of Markets
How Evolution, Psychology, and Biology Have Shaped the Economy
Rojhat Avşar

For more information about this series, please visit: https://www.routledge.com/Economics-as-Social-Theory/book-series/EAST

The Evolutionary Origins of Markets

How Evolution, Psychology, and Biology Have Shaped the Economy

Rojhat Avşar

Routledge
Taylor & Francis Group
LONDON AND NEW YORK

First published 2020
by Routledge
2 Park Square, Milton Park, Abingdon, Oxon OX14 4RN

and by Routledge
52 Vanderbilt Avenue, New York, NY 10017

Routledge is an imprint of the Taylor & Francis Group, an informa business

British Library Cataloguing-in-Publication Data
A catalogue record for this book is available from the British Library

Library of Congress Cataloging-in-Publication Data
Names: Avşar, Rojhat, 1979- author.
Title: The evolutionary origins of markets : how evolution, psychology and biology have shaped the economy / Rojhat Avşar.
Identifiers: LCCN 2019029102 (print) | LCCN 2019029103 (ebook)
Subjects: LCSH: Evolutionary economics. | Economics—Psychological aspects
Classification: LCC HB97.3 .A97 2020 (print) | LCC HB97.3 (ebook) | DDC 330.1—dc23
LC record available at https://lccn.loc.gov/2019029102
LC ebook record available at https://lccn.loc.gov/2019029103

ISBN: 978-0-8153-8718-3 (hbk)
ISBN: 978-0-8153-8719-0 (pbk)
ISBN: 978-1-351-17376-6 (ebk)

Typeset in Palatino
by Thomson Digital

Dedicated to Songül and Hüsamettin

Contents

Acknowledgments

This book would not have seen the light of day without the support and endless encouragement of my wonderful wife, Şule.

This project has forced me to venture into a literature to which I had previously very little exposure. I am indebted to my colleagues Steve Asma and Rami Gabriel for their counsel when I found myself in uncharted territories.

Many thanks to Andy Humphries for believing in the relevance and the timeliness of the topic.

A significant chunk of this book was written at the Peet's Coffee Shop on Elm Street in Winnetka, IL during the early morning hours. I am grateful for the friendly atmosphere created by the baristas, Joel, Maira, Susana, Sarah, and Natalie.

I am grateful to Dustin Meriwether for his assistance in helping me make the text more accessible to a larger audience.

Introduction

As economists, we sometimes tend to lose sight of what our subject matter truly is: human behavior. We study human behavior in isolation, in groups, in organizational settings, and in terms of collective manifestations. The regularities we seek in (and sometimes impose on) the data help us construct narratives. It is not uncommon for quantitative economists to be asked what the "story" behind their numbers is. Humans are the protagonists in all social phenomena, regardless of whether we explicitly recognize it or not. Of course, economists have not been completely blind to the "human" component of their subject matter. Various attempts such as building micro-foundations, representative agents, agent-based modeling, more inclusive utility functions, evolutionary game theory, and so on are all manifestations of the desire among economists to link collective (at macro- or meso-level) outcomes to individual decisions or characteristics.

As a curious mind, I have always appreciated the complexity of the forces behind the human motivation and the susceptibility our brains to the context-specific cues. Behavioral economics has made significant inroads in identifying the consequences of our inherent psychological biases. The distinction the evolutionary theorist makes between "proximate" and "ultimate" causes deeply resonates with me because the rock-bottom explanations, I feel, require a more etiological attitude toward human behavior. We need more "origin" stories. In this sense, sociobiology and its intellectual descendant, evolutionary psychology, with all their alleged reductionist tendencies, offered a breath of fresh air for scholars interested in a robust evolutionary framework in which the universals of social behavior could be studied. Humans are inherently capable of doing certain things like suckling and predisposed to quickly learn to do other things like speaking a language. However, they may not be instructed to fear, for instance, puppies, as easily as they learn to fear snakes. Once we recognize these innate tendencies, it becomes apparent that we are an intelligent species because our brain comes equipped with a large array of pre-built "reasoning instincts" (Tooby and Cosmides, 2015) evolved to solve the recurring adaptive problems faced by our ancestors.

One of the most convincing pieces of evidence for the existence of such innate reasoning instincts comes from, of all places, physics. Specifically, it is possible for us to be very skilled early on at interacting with the physical world, while some of our intuitive predictions about physical events (e.g., trajectory of objects) could also be off by a wide margin (Gerstenberg and Tenenbaum, 2017). Even as infants, we have a certain set of expectations regarding how physical objects should behave—an innate skill that gets even more sophisticated with age. For instance, a five-month-old would probably show signs of confusion if a solid object like a ball was to pass through another solid object like a wall (Hesbos and vanMarle, 2012). However, our intuitive belief about motion may become maladaptive when our predictions systematically deviate from those of classical physics. For instance, when a group of undergraduate students were asked to walk across a room and drop a golf ball at a target marked on the floor, about half the subjects released the ball when it was directly above the mark. This means they failed to understand the role a carried object's initial motion (forward in this case) plays in determining its path when it is dropped, just as an inexperienced basketball player systematically shoots the ball much too hard when they drive toward the basket. Even more interestingly, McCloskey (1983) found that this innate bias could potentially be unlearned since those who have taken at least one physics course at the college level were much more likely to release the ball before (73 percent versus 13) as they should.

Our evolved psychology inevitably shapes what we learn and how we think today. What we learn and how we think, in turn, influence the kind of beliefs and attitudes that disseminate and stick around. I believe explanations ignorant of these connections would leave much of human behavior unaccounted for. Cultures, by virtue of being capable of adapting to our environment much faster than our genotype (our genes), are subject to the same evolutionary pressures—natural selection—as our genes. Genes and culture have been co-evolving, as a result, because there is a feedback loop from cultural invention like animal herding and the human genotype like lactose tolerance. Which genetic dispositions will be favored by natural selection depends on the social and physical environment, which is partly created by us. As Deacon (1998) suggested, for instance, the first use of symbolic reference, thanks to the emergence of verbal language, by some distant ancestors changed how natural selection processes have affected hominid brain evolution ever since. Based on similar and highly plausible cases for the co-evolution thesis, I tend to think of any claims about the direction of potential causation between our biology and culture as dubious at best. Rather, by creating the context for natural selection of our genes, culture has shaped our innate tendencies as much as the other way around. Human cultures are inherent in human biology in the sense that our innate predispositions, like greeting a smile with a smile, and organic constraints, like being unable to breathe under water, influence the (i) ideas that we find attractive, (ii) the skills that we can easily learn, and (iii) the emotions that we can spontaneously experience.

What do I mean by "rock-bottom" explanations? Let me elaborate by revisiting the research question Nisbett and Cohen (1996) tackled in their book, Culture of Honor: "Why do Southerners seem more violent than other Americans in situations that involve personal honor?" "Of course, because of the unique culture of honor prevalent in the South," you might reply. You would be right, but this would only be a proximate cause/explanation for the phenomenon. For a definitive explanation, we may have to get our hands dirty and dig into the cultural and economic histories of the region. Once we begin studying the origin of the first settlers in this region, the first relevant piece of evidence stands out: the American South happened to be the preferred destination for the Irish-Scottish livestock herders (and the North for English, German, and Dutch peasant farmers). What difference does this finding make? As Nisbett and Cohen go on to persuasively argue, for herding societies a culture of honor must have often emerged as a necessity as herders seek to cultivate reputations for willingly resorting to violence as a deterrent to theft and other predatory behavior.

This historical account shows us that the beliefs and attitudes regulating social relations are capable of getting culturally acquired; traveling long distances; and remaining alive and well over many generations. If you feel this sounds like an "ultimate enough" explanation, I am afraid, we are not there yet. So, why do Southerners need a culture of honor? Richerson and Boyd (2005) provided a plausible response informed by the co-evolutionary perspective summarized above: "Perhaps because on average, human males are neither innately sufficiently sensitive to insults nor sufficiently ready to respond violently to them in an environment where self-help violence is the chief means of protecting one's livelihood." (p. 6) That said, they are innately capable of producing cultural norms that prove to be adaptive in their respective environments as they are selected for the reproductive success they bestow on its practitioners.

This co-evolutionary approach does not prioritize one process or the other, as it would be practically a meaningless proposition to make. So, in each case some combination of biological forces and environmental influences constitute the "ultimate" causes of human behavior. The strongest evidence for this position, in my opinion, comes from twin studies. In one such study, the researchers surveyed food preferences among identical and non-identical (dizygotic) twin children. They found that the dislike for food items that are novel (or that children see very rarely), called neophobia, are genetically inheritable to a large extent at about 70 percent (Cooke, Haworth, Wardle, 2007, and Knaapila et al., 2007). But there is more. Food preferences of young children also prove to be malleable in the sense that a combination of modeling and taste exposure earlier in life can help reduce or even reverse the dislike for a particular food item (Wardle and Cooke, 2008). A set of other twin studies show that when growing up in different environments, the identical twins develop similar, as well as distinct, attitudes pointing to a strong gene-environment interaction. Ferguson (2010) surveyed a vast number of studies that focused on the genetic inheritability of antisocial behavior (e.g., aggression, lying, stealing, etc.) based on twin studies. These studies seem to confirm that genetic influences account for the largest component of the variance in anti-social behavior (around 56 percent) with unique non-genetic influences (i.e., the environment) explaining about 31 percent. The fact that genetic inheritability is more visible among the younger participants provides further scientific backing for the gene-environment interaction thesis as we expect the influence the environment exerts to gradually grow stronger later in life.

It is probably becoming, perhaps, a bit clearer by now why I find the sociobiological approach promising for studying economic behavior. Let me offer the following demonstration to further elaborate the value and usefulness I attribute to this particular approach to social behavior. The hypothetical scenario below is a slight variation on the Fable of Two Goats and a Bridge with which I am familiar from my own childhood. In the fable, our protagonists find themselves in a coordination dilemma that economists often study in game theory. The two goats face each other on a bridge only wide enough for a single goat to cross at a time. Neither goat intends to yield. As they power their way by one another, both fall to the river underneath. After this episode has been replicated a few times, the goats come to their senses and choose to communicate/cooperate with one of them yielding. The moral of the story that we would like our children to take away from this story is obvious. Additionally, the fable rings true—it's not uncommon for animals to learn from their past experiences even though they may not have the capacity to transmit that knowledge to their offspring. For instance, Clayton, Bussey, and Dickinson (2003) found that western scrub-jays, a bird species, not only possess episodic memory, but are able to apply episodic memory flexibly in novel situations.

My interest in the fable lies elsewhere: the situation lends itself to a game theoretical analysis. On the surface, it is a simple coordination game analogous to an intersection regulated by four-way stop signs. But what happens, as seems to be the case in our fable, if the goats arrive at the bridge at the same time with no clear guidance as to who has the right of way? If yielding is not reciprocated in the next round, the relationship is no longer one of equality. As a result, cooperation is likely to stop unless the original yielder accepts the other party's dominance—a behavior that is not uncommon among goats that feature a unique pecking order of their own. Such a hierarchical solution would not be limited to goats, either, and may prove to be adaptive. In fact, hierarchy emerged as a coordination tool among human societies as well. In this context, submission functions as a form of cooperation.

Under the usual assumption we make in game theoretical situations—that both parties are equal and rational—we expect them to calculate the cooperative outcome to be in their best interest and reciprocate appropriately in (infinitely) repeated interactions. As a result, reciprocal yielding emerges as a social norm, which is culturally transmitted from across generations. Viola! I would like to call this line of thinking the "they would just figure it out" approach. But I am not convinced by the plausibility of this account, as it offers a too flimsy foundation for cooperation to emerge in evolutionary time.

The following account, I believe, would offer a much more plausible story: goats that fall to their demise will not be represented in the future gene pool from that point forward. Only those that are genetically inclined to cooperate (e.g., even-tempered and farsighted ones) would. Such cooperation-friendly traits spread out over time such that cooperation becomes instinctively rewarding—assuming the environmental backdrop against which the natural selection is operating is static enough. If we would like to know why modern goats display cooperative tendencies, we need to account for the adaptive pressures from their environment and conspecifics imposed on their ancestors. This is what evolutionary psychology, one of the intellectual descendants of sociobiology (see Griffiths, 2007, for a more detailed account of the history of the field) offers. In a nutshell, the evolutionary psychologists argued that if we can figure out what adaptive problems our foraging ancestors faced on the African savannahs, we can make some educated guesses about the kind of mental adaptations that natural selection might have produced to solve them. For example, since our ancestors lived in tightly-knit communities because of the advantages in catching prey and providing defense, social environment (our relationship with our conspecifics) probably posed at least as many (if not more) problems for ancestors as their physical environment did. The ability to form alliances/coalitions and friendships became a matter of survival. Many of our natural cooperative inclinations such as reciprocal altruism could be considered positively selected adaptations because of their role in alliance formation. Moreover, our hunter-gatherer ancestors developed complex rituals with no apparent survival benefits for the individual. The primary function of these rituals was to facilitate effective cooperation and reinforce social cohesion (Henrich, 2015). Similarly, as Wilson suggested, egalitarian ethos may have become part of our genetic endowment for similar purposes. Modern concepts like health insurance resemble our inclination to share big game regardless of who hunted it to compensate for variations in hunting success and the pressures of the, what Charlton (1997) called, "immediate-return economy."

At this point a gentle warning is in order about the terminology, as I understand it. My approach draws on evolutionary psychology both in

the strict and the broad sense of the term as distinguished in the literature (Kopppl, 2004). The former is grounded in the modularity thesis popularized by Barkow, Cosmides, and Tooby (1995). The latter refers to any theory or argument that draws conclusions about human psychology from man's evolutionary history. The practitioners of both fields are united in their belief that our evolutionary "baggage" is still exercising a strong pull on our behavior—a position that I adopt.

Let me provide some examples for how our evolutionary heritage manifests itself in modern life. In his rebuttal to those who blame obesity on a lack of self-control, Ubel points out that our ancestors would have probably gorged themselves on the kill in good times, storing meat in their own fat cells and glycogen stores. Evolution must have favored those individuals who could conserve energy (by getting fat!) and thereby hold on to the calories they had already consumed. Since our ancestors confronted a situation in which food arrives sporadically, this was an adaptive biological response. By storing food internally and carrying it forward, to be used at times when no food is available, we increased our expected total number of offspring. Even if storage involves a metabolic cost, as Robson (2002) argued, it would still be favored (almost as a form of self-insurance) if the cost is not too large. Apparently, we have not evolved to be successful dieters, just like we have not evolved to be successful savers or probability experts. Our basic nutritional preferences are also shaped biologically as our genome remains largely adapted for the Paleolithic existence. We all have the inclination to find foods high in fat, salt, and sugar pleasurable and we find exercise generally displeasurable. The explanations for these tendencies lie in our evolutionary heritage. Polyunsaturated fatty acids and sodium are required nutrients, but on the African savanna they were most likely in scarce supply, so taste preferences for them were advantageous. And there must have been an active selection against wasting calories on unproductive exercise (Eaton et al., 2002).

I find it very encouraging as a social scientist that the human mind is no longer the enigma that it once was. Advances in the sciences of human nature (with all of their methodological limitations) have enabled us to supplement the useful experimental evidence coming from behavioral studies and acquire a much deeper insight as to the forces behind human behavior and motivation. In this book, I will try to integrate the growing body of experimental evidence on human nature scattered across a variety of disciplines from experimental economics to social neuroscience into a coherent and, hopefully, an original narrative about the extent to which market (or impersonal exchange) relations are reflective of the basic human sociality that was originally adapted to a more tribal existence. By articulating the relevance of the innate human sociality for building an extensive network of impersonal exchange populated with individuals and organizations, I hope to be able to formulate a set of substantive and fresh responses to the following questions:

- In which sense are exchange relations embedded in social relations?
- Can profit-seeking organization exist without co-opting social norms?
- In which sense do consumption and employment represent realms where Sapiens may be exercising their sociality?

My approach to these questions builds on several convictions based on my reading of the existing literature: First, evolutionary psychology is capable of providing a plausible theoretical framework with testable predictions in which the human social behavior could be systematically studied. However, the field is dominated by cognitive scientists and the role of affect has not been given the consideration it deserves. Second, emotions and affect are keys to social interactions and underlie the functioning of the "automatic system" in the brain that guides a significant portion of our daily social life. Third, social neuroscience, a relatively new field, provides the necessary experimental evidence to corroborate many of the predictions produced by evolutionary psychology. Lastly, the advances in neuroscientific methodology do not make behavioral experiments obsolete. On the contrary, the growing knowledge of the brain's anatomy and experimental social psychology supplement one another in powerful ways. My approach is eclectic in the sense that it draws on all behavioral, affective, and cognitive dimensions of social behavior.

Part I

Social brain

1 The myth of the dissociative identities

In the movie *Me, Myself, and Irene,* Charlie, played by Jim Carey, is known for his friendly, gentle, caring, and somewhat passive personality and finds himself often getting ridiculed by his colleagues as a result. Under socially stressful situations, Charlie transforms into Hank, his other personality. In terms of personality, Hank could not be more different from Charlie: Hank is assertive, aggressive, and much more hedonistic. Moreover, he does not follow social conventions. Charlie, as you might be able to tell by now, suffers from dissociative identity disorder, which is characterized by the presence of two or more distinct (or split) identities or personality states that continually compete for power over the person's behavior. Charlie seems to oscillate between these two extreme personalities.

Most economists seem to believe that we act as if we have a split personality, of the kind similar to the one described above. As the belief goes, we can separate market relations from the rest of our social life with a great ease, behaving differently—sometimes surprisingly so—in each domain. From this perspective, seamlessly navigating our way back and forth between personal exchange (e.g., friendship) and financial transactions (e.g., taking out a mortgage) is our second nature. On the surface, this seems like a commonsensical approach: the domain where people engage in exchange or cooperation for strictly personal gains must naturally be regulated by a different set of norms. That is why the introduction of financial incentives might possibly change how a particular exchange or interaction is perceived, particularly one that is more purely social. For example, when Greg Rosalsky, a producer at Freakonomics Radio, offered money to get people on the New York subway train yield their seats to him, he received interesting and varied reactions, suggesting that he violated the expectations of that situation by interjecting money into an interaction that is regulated by social norms—that is, regulated by currencies other than money. Some of the fellow commuters were simply puzzled by the very suggestion, while others indicated that they might be willing to move from their seats only for considerations other than money (e.g., injury, age, etc.). Others yet were downright hostile.

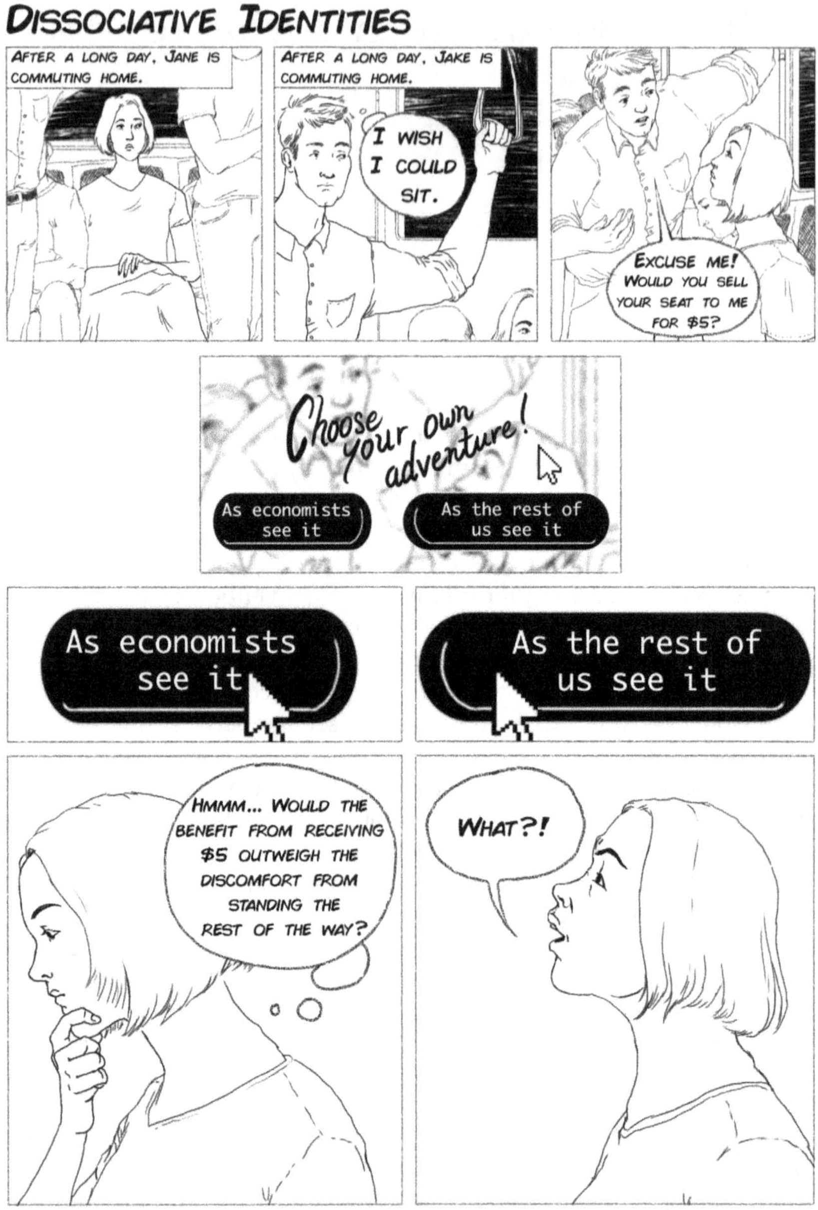

While this is perhaps a surprising finding, given that one might expect people to accept such easily obtained money, Vohs and her colleagues (2006) predicted that this would happen, albeit indirectly. They found that reminders of money would lead to behavior changes that suggest a feeling of self-sufficiency, indicated by the relative reluctance to ask help. When people are primed to think about money (i.e., when sub- or supraliminal experimental techniques are used to trigger conscious or subconscious thoughts about money), they more strongly prefer to be free from dependency; both in terms of depending on others and in terms of having others depend on them. For example, they were less helpful (in terms of time commitment) when asked for help and they donated less when solicited. These findings provide a strong example of how monetary considerations can overwhelm or crowd-out social considerations (Bowles & Polania-Reyes, 2012). That is why it is not often that we find ourselves offering to compensate our hosts for their trouble at a Thanksgiving dinner.

For another example, consider the day care center in Israel that, in attempts to rein in the late pickups, introduced a financial penalty (disincentive) and charged tardy parents a fee. One would expect that the parents would make better attempts at punctuality to avoid the penalty. Not so. The fine actually led to a substantial increase in the frequency of late pick-ups. The introduction of money (i.e., a fine) into a normally purely social situation apparently transformed the parents' view of their efforts from one of generosity and duty (a non-market activity) to a mere service with a price attached to it (a market activity), thereby eliminating any sense of guilt that might normally accompany violation of social expectations.

The most bipolar ape

Although I seem to have been, so far, trying to convince you to believe otherwise, we do indeed have a split personality, in a manner of speaking. Its behavioral manifestation, however, does not map onto the market vs. social relations dichotomy and is much more nuanced and deep-seated. To understand this "bipolar" tendency, Cory's (2006) dual motive theory, built upon Maclean's triune brain model, is particularly promising, as it links the neural architecture of our brain, which has evolved in a layered fashion, to the broad range of social exchange relationships in which we can engage. According to the triune brain model, the human brain has evolved to consist of a three-level interconnected structure: (i) a self-preservational, maintenance component inherited from the stem reptiles, called the proto-reptilian complex; (ii) the mammalian affectional complex; and (iii) the most recent higher cortex. In other words, the brain structures of early vertebrate life forms ancestral to humans (i.e., early fishes and reptiles) became the substructures for later iterations, the foundation on which mammalian and neocortical elaborations have been built.

Based on the Maclean's typology, it makes sense to frame, as Cory did, human behavior in terms of an ongoing tension between two conflicting motives, self-interest (or ego) and other-interest (empathy), that originate in two separate motivational circuits in the brain. Self-interested motives are instrumental in achieving basic self-preservation-related objectives and are supported by the most ancient (i.e., proto-reptilian) circuits. Other-interested preferences are associated with the affectional (i.e., mammalian) circuits that were integrated later in the evolutionary process. In this framework, the new kid on the block—that is, the frontal cortex—is charged with the unenviable task of mediating the opposing demands of these circuits. This dynamic interaction produces a wide range of possible behavioral outcomes, from self-sacrifice at one extreme, where empathy dominates, to aggressiveness at the opposite extreme, where egotistic motives win over. Both cases tend to generate a perceptible behavioral tension or a form of disequilibrium. Such unresolved tension, when it accumulates, will prove to be disruptive for the individual (e.g., feeling anxious) and the group (e.g., animosity toward others). A more balanced behavioral outcome would be characterized by a compromise between the extremes, where both the respect for both oneself and for others are present, such as is observed in a reciprocal social exchange situation where favors of (approximately) equal quantity are being swapped either simultaneously or in succession.

One of the implications of the dual motive theory is that we have a social brain that equips us with the capability to reconcile the basic self-preservational imperatives with the demands of social interactions. The self-interested (self-preservational) and other-regarding (affective) motivation are both key to social exchange. This characterization is similar to the way in which the impartial spectator modulates our passions, as argued by Adam Smith in his Theory of the Moral Sentiments. Although it is possible to be paralyzed by the opposing promptings of self-preservation and affection ("I want to but I can't"), they are often combined to give us a rich behavioral repertoire the enables us, for instance, to quickly empathize (at least verbally) with a fuming customer to set a softer tone for the rest of our conversation. In this sense, envisioning the market realm as a space for purely self-interested pursuits seems to be an empty—or at least an incomplete—proposition to make. Every social exchange situation is potentially fraught with this preservation-empathy tension, from romantic relationships to trade, making us act in rather odd, bipolar ways—sometimes Charlie, sometimes as Hank. As such, to better understand market relationships and the full richness of economic behavior, we must consider this bipolar tension within us and appreciate the craftiness its takes to mold these opposite forces into a ecologically rational behavioral patterns.

Born to barter?

The account I put forth takes a different approach to this ability of ours to adapt to the market exchange and organize ourselves into abstract organizations despite of both institutions' quick rise to being the prominent mode of interaction today among strangers. The conflation examples

cited in the beginning of this chapter show that when we insert monetary considerations into a set of interactions that are typically governed by social "currencies" (i.e., norms, expectations), the outcome is unsettling. However, the inverse, invoking social norms in the market setting, is not only much less problematic, but is also, in some cases, inevitable. How so?

Isn't market exchange the domain of purely disinterested and calculated exchange? Not really, as I hinted above. Market exchange presupposes and, to some extent, facilitates various forms of human sociality. I will elaborate more on this argument in Chapter 9, but for now, let me just state that social exchange is ancient, while market exchange is in its infancy. Furthermore, while the latter was born out of the former, both forms of interactions draw on the same set of social competencies, which will be the focus of the rest of this chapter.

One thing that sets humans apart from other species is the frequency of mutually beneficial interactions in which we engage where one party provides a benefit to the other conditional on the recipient's providing a benefit in return (more on this in Chapter 5). Moreover, we engage in various forms of this kind of social exchange, from simultaneous to sequential, from explicit to implicit, and more. Simultaneous exchange of objects (as opposed to favors or help) based on an explicit agreement is more likely to occur between individuals who are socially distant. This is the type of exchange that economists study. Anthropologists, on the other hand, are more interested in the kind of exchange situations that are implicit and that lack immediacy.

Social exchange, as Cosmides and Tooby (2015) put it, is ubiquitously woven through the fabric of humanity, exists in all human cultures everywhere, and has been taking place since the time of our ancestors, for at least a few millions of years, while even earlier forms of social exchange probably existed before the hominid line split from the chimpanzees. This network of mutual obligations, whether giving of meat or aid, helped to sustain our ancestors. Such interactions, being an important and recurrent human activity over such a long time scale, have come to create special neural adaptations. Thus, what Adam Smith calls the "propensity to barter" would not have come about unless *Homo sapiens* had a set of neural networks specialized for social exchange, thereby enabling them to engage in the effective reciprocal relationships which characterized and sustained their foraging, small-band lifestyle. As Polanyi (1957) suggests in Great Transformation, we would be helped tremendously in our pursuit of explaining fundamental problems of economic and social history, such as the origin of fluctuating prices and the development of market trading, if we begin with non-financially motivated concepts of trade, money, and market. In other words, our ability to establish equivalencies, which must underlie any market exchange, has ancient roots.

Although our species has been bartering (and, later on, buying and selling) for a long time, this activity was a relatively insignificant detail in our social lives up until recent centuries. The previous economic systems (i.e., systems of production, distribution, etc.) that existed, as Polanyi argues, had to run on non-economic motives (e.g., group solidarity) to a large extent. Perhaps one of the most clear-cut examples of this phenomenon (one of many which Jared Diamond supplies in The World Until Yesterday) is that some traditional societies that were otherwise self-sufficient often chose to acquire some objects by trade instead of by producing them for themselves in order to maintain their relationships with the neighboring tribes and to form political alliances (e.g., Momaribowei-teri villagers and the trade of pots). In other words, we as a species have long understood that, as Sahlins (2017) succinctly puts it, "If friends make gifts, gifts make friends" (p. 186). Some cultures even make it a point to exaggerate the friendliness of these exchanges. For instance, although Kung has very strong gift-exchange customs (that sometimes involve asking), to test each other's resolve to stay on good terms, they deliberately delay reciprocating a gift so that the exchange would not look like trading. Even when the trade aimed for mutual gains driven by comparative advantages (e.g., surplus), lacking a middleman, it often resembled a (reciprocal) gift exchange wherein the recipient was expected to provide a good of equal value in return sometime down the road (and very rarely simultaneously as is the case with the market exchange). In contrast to these relationship-based exchanges, most modern market exchanges feature users and buyers with little to no personal relationship beyond the current transaction. Yet the social roots of these interactions still influence behavior in such exchanges. In fact, I would like to convince you, social factors are much stronger than we used to think.

Instinctively social

We, *Homo sapiens*, have interacted with our brethren in various contexts with accelerated frequency owing to population growth and transition to a more settled lifestyle with the advent of agriculture. As a result, we have developed a specific set of social instincts that are indispensable for an effective and a sustained cooperation. As de Waal sums up in Our Inner Ape (2005), the origin stories, such as Ken Binmore's (1994) game-theoretic approach (e.g., Folk Theorem) to the evolution of social norms, that present humans as loners who grudgingly came together are ignorant of primate evolution. The use of infinitely played games as a metaphor for the evolution of human cooperation is problematic at best, because the (pre-social) "state of nature" they presuppose never existed. The explanation provided for the natural emergence of social norms from a supposedly a pre-social state has always struck me as deeply flawed. Although it helps to expand the domain of what constitutes the "rational" behavior," game theory (if we leave out studies based on replicator dynamics) does not strike me as a plausible model for modeling the emergence of the basic pro-social attitudes.

When referring to human social interactions, the term "social instinct" is quite an apt descriptor, because our inclination to cooperate (and to punish opportunists) is supported and reinforced by our affective make-up (e.g., anger felt in the face of unfair treatment) and cannot be explained by our sophisticated cognitive faculties alone—that is, it is quite instinctive behavior. (I will expand on this in Chapter 4.) Therefore, we should consider these social instincts, which underlie our cooperative ability, as a form of "competence without comprehension" (Dennett, 2018) that reflects the "intelligence of our unconscious" (Gigerenzer & Rossbach, 2008) (more on this in Chapter 3). Therefore, as Gintis (2006) points out, it is much more plausible to argue that human beings are emotionally constituted to adopt prosocial and altruistic notions of reciprocity. In other words, cooperation puts us in a pleasant emotional state. Seabright (2011) offers a similar explanation in his quest to explain how a web of collaboration among strangers could be compatible with our so-called stone-age brain: "Cooperation is shaped by our emotions as well as by our capacity to calculate, and understanding our emotions is as important for cooperation as understanding our cognitive faculties" (p. 131). That fact that we feel anger when norms are violated (Fehr & Gachter, 2002) or when we are cheated in an economic exchange (Cohen and Dickens, 2002) is a perfect case in point.

Evolutionary psychologists like, Cosmides, Barret, and Tooby, building on the sociobiology revolution, were among the first to study these social instincts and were the first to forcefully argue for the existence of so called "social contract algorithms" (2010, 2015). Such algorithms are argued to be supported by a set of (probably designated) neural circuitry in the brain, and their emergence has a lot to do with our lifestyle in cooperative small groups and our long history as a species of social exchange:

> the enduring presence of social exchange interactions among our ancestors has selected for cognitive mechanisms that are specialized for reasoning about social exchange. Just as a lock and key are designed to fit together to function, our claim is that the proprietary procedures and conceptual elements of the social exchange reasoning specializations evolved to reflect the abstract, evolutionarily recurring relationships present in social exchange interactions (Cosmides & Tooby, 2015, p. 626).

These algorithms can be best described as social reasoning instincts and can include such things, as gauging others' desires, intentions, and motives, often effortlessly. We have many such specialized instincts to deal with various problems, and the absence of such instincts appears to cause serious social disadvantages. Consider the following scenario. A kindergartener—let's call her Julia—is presented with a few candy options to choose from, all laid out on the table before her. Her classmates are asked to guess which candy she is likely to choose. This is an elaborate mind-reading exercise. Children with autism, who have difficulty mentalizing (i.e., guessing the thoughts and intentions of others), guess randomly as to which candy she'll pick. They are unable to associate her gaze direction with her intention. Others are able read Julia's mind from her gaze and correctly guess that she is likely to choose the candy she is looking at. (For variations of this experiment, see Baron-Cohen et al., 1995). Evolutionary psychologists believe that human social intelligence is made up of many such innate competencies, most of which are performed unconsciously. I argue in the next chapter (and in this book, in general) that a significant chunk of these natural skills evolved to accommodate the demands of our complex social life and constitute the basis for our ability to engage in impersonal exchange.

Evolutionary psychology also provides a plausible link between our evolved nature and the widespread existence of social norms. The constellation of rules, norms, and institutions that we call culture has certain intelligence inherent in it, even though, in most cases, it is not a product of any individual's deliberate design. Yet it is a product of the design—and needs—of its individuals. Cultures exist because their norms provide us with what Henrich (2015) refers to as protocols (i.e., pre-built solutions) that allow us to not have to approach every decision as though it were a brand-new experience. Neurally, these protocols come about as a result of the brain's tendency to be efficient in the sense that it avoids spending more energy than necessary. Because our brains are able to process things unconsciously and simultaneously, we can go about our daily lives without needing to engage in continuous monitoring and conscious control of our decisions (Smith, 2008). Thus, we come to learn and rely on protocols, such as cultural norms, freeing out cognitive energies for other important decisions, tasks, and activities. The world in which you have to figure out whether or not to hold the door for the next person each time you face this situation would be simply unmanageable and overwhelming! Because of how ingrained—and in the brain—these social protocols are, we need to consider their effect on interpersonal exchanges, even impersonal ones.

Oldest currency: reputation

Human sociality, however, has received scant attention as a primary driver of our species' success, even though we have a very long history of social exchange and specialization. We care deeply about how we are perceived by others, and, as a result, are highly receptive to social influence and instruction, even though we can't clearly appreciate the fitness benefits of such behavior—a trait which Herbert Simon (1990) called "docility." Why has such a trait been positively selected? We can consider reputation, which spread initially via word-of-mouth, as the world's oldest currency. While not tangible in the way other currencies are, reputation is a currency in the sense that we are able to earn, accumulate, and spend it. Moreover, with the diffusion of human languages, reputation has become transferrable (as we expect from any currency), thereby allowing traits such as kindness and honesty, among others, to play to a much larger audience than merely those who witness such actions (Pagel, 2013). Without this currency, there would have probably been no decentralized (i.e., bottom-up) and cost-efficient checks on violations of cultural norms. When reciprocal cooperation generates a net return for the parties involved, Ostrom argues, there will be an incentive to develop a reputation for keeping promises and performing actions with immediate costs but long-term net benefits:

> Thus, trustworthy individuals who trust others with a reputation for being trustworthy (and try to avoid those who have a reputation for being untrustworthy) can engage in mutually productive social exchanges, even though they are dilemmas, so long as they can limit their interactions primarily to those with a reputation for keeping promises. A reputation for being trustworthy, or for using retribution against those who do not keep their agreements or keep up their fair share, becomes a valuable asset. In an evolutionary context, it increases fitness in an environment in which others use reciprocity norms. Similarly, developing trust in an environment in which others are trustworthy is also an asset. (1998, p. 12).

Given the importance of this currency of reputation and all the interpersonal and intercultural benefits it affords, human societies developed defenses against the disorderly conduct from within their own ranks as a means of protecting reputation. The first line of defense became gossip. It helped detect social deviants and maintain a dossier of information on individual members of the group. As Wilson puts it, gossip functions very much like an immune system, aiding the creation of a social environment in which genuine trustworthiness and altruism can thrive, precisely because the wolves of selfishness are being held at bay. Credit card reports, online ratings, and background checks are mere modern incarnations of the key social database once maintained by our collective memory.

Retaliation comes in where gossip fails, one of two additional mechanisms that Bowles and Gintis (2012) argue have been key to the emergence and the sustenance of communities as viable economic units. When agents engage in repeated interaction in small groups, they will have many incentives to build and protect their reputation for cooperative behavior. The incentive to act favorably toward one's partners, they argue, will be reinforced by the fact that there might be opportunities for retaliation against opportunistic behavior later on. Perhaps, as the size of human groups expanded, the institutionalization of retaliation, or "a social of division of sanction" (Dubreuil, 2008), became a pre-requisite for the social integration at a larger scale. The second key mechanism is segmentation effects. In the company of like-minded partners, pro-social traits are more likely to pay off and increase the frequency of such encounters (the segmentation effect). Over time, such attitudes will be diffused and replicated as they prove to be successful.

In light of all this, reputation is not only a plausible, but a much more inclusive, explanation than kin selection (i.e., the family first mentality) for why we engage in the seemingly counterintuitive (from a natural selection standpoint) strong altruism—even with strangers in one-off interactions—from which we do not stand to gain immediately. Reputation points earned through costly public displays of civic-mindedness could be redeemed for the trust and the cooperation of others, allowing us to go beyond the limits of kin-based partnerships.

We should also highlight another, and perhaps a more cynical, aspect of our ability to engage in beneficent actions toward non-kin, one with roots lying in cultural evolution, namely, that we are motivated to increase our cultural fitness. From this point of view, we are more likely to display altruism toward our cultural associates (be it your neighbor or parents) and those who exhibit particular cultural markers (Allison, 1992). This bias perhaps stems from our ability to make "us vs. them" distinctions (which is often employed in the organizational setting, as I will discuss in the final chapter). The fact that even babies display favoritism based on even the most arbitrary markers (Hamlin et al., 2013) should tell us that this inclination comes to us naturally and must have been adaptive in the ancestral environment.

Lastly, although we share the same set of psychological adaptations as a species, there are significant individual variations in the way cooperative attitudes are distributed. For instance, in experiments examining prosocial behavior, participants can be grouped into three broad personality types based on their contribution levels: cooperators who contribute most of the time, reciprocators who contribute if others contribute, and free-riders who contribute rarely, if at all. Kurzban and Houser (2005) found, as one would expect, that the composition of the group (its cooperativeness score) is a great predictor of the group's total contribution at the final stage of a game. These results are interesting for two primary reasons. First, they indicate that, even when the cooperative types are in the majority, cooperative outcomes are not guaranteed. For instance, three reciprocators produce a cooperative outcome when partnered with a cooperator, but will be less cooperative when partnered with a free rider. Secondly, and more importantly, cooperative groups earn substantially more. In the absence of external reinforcement, cooperative outcomes will be context-dependent and fragile. However, repeated personal interactions, not surprisingly, are more conducive for effective and sustained social exchange. Cooperation is key. Since today many of our interactions may not necessarily be characterized as such, we must rely on a set of institutions (from federal mandates to online ratings) to alleviate the potential pitfalls of infrequent and impersonal exchange.

Homo sapiens have managed to create complex social contracts enabling them to engage in two unique kinds of cooperative behavior not seen together elsewhere in nature: reciprocal altruism and strong altruism. Such an extraordinary collaborative acumen requires a high level of psychological sophistication. I intend to investigate this in the following chapters by invoking a recent body of experimental evidence coming from social neuroscience—a field that has made significant contributions to our understanding of the economic functions of human sociality. After all, to understand how we operate in economic situations, we must understand how the brain is operating in us.

2 Why wouldn't chimpanzees wear sunglasses while playing poker?

Why do gorillas need big brains? After all, their daily routine involves a repeated cycle of eating, sleeping, and playing—all done within a mile radius! Moreover, there is no sign that their big brain is being utilized to create any practical inventions, according to observations by Nick Humphrey during his field studies. Like a 2019 Ferrari Spider equipped with a 720-horsepower engine that will never get to 211 mph under the existing speed limits, gorillas certainly seem to be carrying around some excess brainpower.

Social brain theory

Upon closer inspection, the reason why the gorillas' life in the forest seems so mundane to an outsider is primarily because, as Humphrey realized, the gorilla family, as a social unit, is very well adapted to this lifestyle. For instance, many practical skills are handed down from generation to generation. This is what we call social learning.

Moreover, each gorilla intimately knows each other gorilla and, more importantly, his/her place (e.g., grooming orders) in the community. These skills are key to creating and maintaining a stable group. Humphrey goes on to suggest that social intelligence has driven the biological success of great apes, humans included. Particularly, our ability to play the natural psychologist—which exists to a degree in other apes as well—alone demands significant brainpower. Alternatively, consider the dynamic power maneuvers among the chimpanzees, the most extensive account of which has been provided by the primatologist de Waal. These power moves consist of a mix of competitive and cooperative social tactics that are believed to have formed through a "Machiavellian arms races" (Whiten and de Waal, 2017) wherein selection pressures led to a highly sophisticated level of social strategy that is observed only among our closet evolutionary cousins—those also equipped with large brains. As an example, Pawlowski, Lowen, and Dunbar (1998) found that, among promiscuously mating primates, lower-ranked males have access to more mating opportunities the larger the species' brain is.

Humphrey's insight became popular and is known today as the Social Brain Hypothesis, owing to R. I. M. Dunbar's seminal and widely accepted work showing a strong connection between the level of social complexity among primates (particularly those of anthropoid varieties) and the ratio of the size of the neocortex to the rest of the body. Social complexity is a vague term that can refer to various factors, such as the size of the grooming circle, rate of deception, etc. However, the most common measure of social complexity for primates is the size of the group to which they belong. A bigger group means more social connections to keep track of, which requires greater brainpower.

Dunbar's research included another interesting finding: pair-bonded animals have larger brains, a finding that is particularly pronounced among birds. It is fairly easy to imagine the cognitive demands of living in a larger, more complex community, but what is so cognitively challenging about pair-bonded relationships? He cites two possible reasons, but points to the latter being more likely explanation: (1) the pressure to find the most reliable and fertile mate; and (2) the need to coordinate and synchronize behavior on a daily basis. Among the pair bonded monogamists, the cognitive demands reflected in the need to coordinate one's behavior with that of one's mate in meeting nutritional needs, attending to their offspring, etc., were possibly the critical factor responsible for triggering the evolution of large brains in both birds and mammals. Moreover, the ability to sense a mate's needs most likely required perspective-taking skills, a precursor to mentalizing (i.e., perceiving others' thoughts and intentions, as discussed in the previous chapter). The added brain tissue required for such high-level skills consumes much more energy than the equivalent amount of skeletal muscle, so there must have been equivalent and advantageous survival gains for natural selection to opt for such a larger brain. Our unique sociality, afforded by our large brain, seems to be worth it.

Socially sharp

Signs of the social intelligence of our species are everywhere, and there are countless studies in fields ranging from social psychology to neuroscience that reliably capture our social intelligence at work. However, its daily exercise is cognitively impenetrable, to a larger extent. Consider the experiment conducted by Dunn and Seale (2010) in which they manipulated "status" through the implementation of photographic images. Basically, they depicted male and female models seated either in a high status (Silver Bentley Continental GT) or neutral status (Red Ford Fiesta ST) car and asked participants of the opposite sex to rate these models in terms of attractiveness. They found that the male model was rated as significantly more attractive by females, when he was in the high-status car, even though he was photographed in the same clothing and with the same facial expressions in both cars. However, the same status manipulation does not seem to have any effects on the attractiveness ratings of the female model by the male participants.

Walter et al. (2005) conducted a somewhat complementary experiment, but only with male participants. They found that more attractive sports cars elicited stronger activations in several brain regions, including areas implicated in anticipating rewards, suggesting that the participants "wanted" the sport cars more. Why? As superficial as their reaction may appear, it is actually another sign of our mastery of recognizing relevant social cues. The question we need to ask, then, is this: why the sports cars represented as valuable in the mind of the male participants? The researchers propose that sports cars function as a signal of social dominance. As social relationships are very important part of the life of higher mammals (like us), we must have developed the appropriate skills to recognize signals related to social hierarchy and dominance. As a general rule, we seek more status, not less, and this is owing to the earlier motivational adaptations generated by the processes of the Darwinian sexual selection aimed to further reproductive success.

Whether we like or not, our evolution has gifted us with a brain that is obsessed with our social relations and identifying socially relevant information. We find making inferences about other people's state of minds, for strategic or recreational reasons (e.g., gossiping or watching soap operas), to be simply irresistible. Adding grease to the fire, our biology has evolved to make such inferences much easier. For instance, concerning our ability to conceal our inner thoughts, we are at a great disadvantage (at least compared to other primates) by having the most expressive eyes. This is why no primate would find it advantageous to wear sunglasses while playing poker, but a human poker player may opt to do so for strategic reasons (i.e., hiding a tell). If a chimp is looking in a direction other than the one in which their heads are pointing, we have a hard time discerning what they are looking at, as Tomasello (2007) pointed out. In comparison, we are like an open book, due to the fact that the whites of our eyes are several times larger than those of other primates. This has resulted in (or, perhaps, resulted from) the notion that, in humans, eye gaze has evolved as an essential cue to social attention that can be used to detect others' focus of interest in the environment and infer their intentions (Lachat et al., 2012).

Even when we are at "rest" (i.e., not being cognitively occupied with anything in particular), our social brain still seems to be active. In these times of rest, our brain settles in to its rest mode, a process that is supported by what cognitive scientists call the default mode network. This the same network that is usually active in social cognition tasks, like attributing mental states to others (Mars et al., 2012), suggesting that "the brain's baseline activity might reflect a mode of operation that is already tuned to interpreting and categorizing the world as social" (Adolphs, 2003, p. 174). Yet we also take this to the extreme and ascribe socialness to non-social things, such as how we attribute human-like

EASY TO READ

features to inanimate objects. Heider and Simmel (1944), in their classic experiment, had a group of 36 undergraduate students watch a movie of interacting shapes. When the participants were asked to comment on the personality of each shape, they recounted the episode in anthropomorphic terms. The shapes were described as having intentions and qualities, such as aggressive, timid, and brave, among others, that we generally reserve for describing animate beings. The experiment put on full display our tendency to engage in social thinking about natural phenomena, a process through which we infer and respond to the unobservable mental features of non-human agents as human-like. Our styles of thinking, which are primarily suited to social problem solving, color our cognitions and behaviors even toward the inanimate world. The metaphors that commentators use to explain daily patterns of stock prices, is another perfect case in point. For instance, Morris et al. (2007) found that, when stocks are consistently trending upward, commentators tend to describe the price patterns with agent metaphors (e.g., "the NASDAQ climbed higher"), as though the price trajectories were volitional actions and internally driven behaviors of an animate entity. More interestingly, investment behavior appears to be sensitive to such characterizations. Apparently, we are wired to assign meanings and intentions, even when it is clearly non-sensical to do so.

Our social intelligence is supported and maintained by a variety of competencies that come to us naturally and are performed effortlessly. For instance, we have a specialized innate and automatic attention to biological motion (movement like that of living organisms). Specifically, the superior temporal sulcus is argued to be responsible for detecting biological motion in our environment, a process that is integral to social perception (e.g., eye movements). Even newborns display a preference for biological motion (Simion et al., 2001), suggesting that, even from birth, we are dialed in to socially relevant stimuli, whether visual, auditory, or other. Since it is highly critical for social interaction to know the emotional state of the other party, we must be good at reading other emotional cues, particularly, from facial expressions; thankfully, we are, as many experimental studies using eye-tracking technology have shown. Autistic individuals, however, appear to display diminished gaze fixation and show less than normal activation in the fusiform gyrus (Dalton et al., 2005), the brain region that plays important roles in object and face recognition, including recognition of facial expressions. Eisenbarth and Alpers (2011) studied where we fixate our gaze first in decoding particular emotional expressions, findings that the eyes and mouth appear to be key regions for carrying emotion-specific information. We tend to assess someone's happiness, they found, by initially fixating on their mouth, while we look more to the eyes to tell us about sadness, with anger lying somewhere in between.

Now, consider how we might measure the trustworthiness of a potential exchange partner—a skill that must come in handy when dealing with strangers in one-off economic transactions. In a recent study, Centorrino and his colleagues (2015) focused on our inherent tendency to associate genuine smiles with a trustworthy character. They not only found that we are more likely to trust those who are able to sport a more genuine smile, but also that we would, on average, be justified in doing so. Those who participated in this trust experiment sent more money to those whose smiles were rated as more genuine; those whose smiles were rated as more genuine sent more money back to the senders. Thus, the ability to recognize a genuine smile and use the simple heuristic of assessing trustworthiness by the genuineness of the smile seems to have paid off for those who followed it—at least in this experiment. Although such experiments do show our overt sensitivity to social cues, we should not be quick to generalize the findings of these experiments. Most importantly, I do not think believe we are a good judge of one's moral character at a first pass. Relying on snap judgments in choosing a cooperation partners would not have been evolutionarily stable strategy as it would be vulnerable to those who can fake these gestures. That is, perhaps, why we need to rely on us-them distinctions based on arbitrary markers (e.g., clothing style). In other cases, we have to wait until our potential partners to prove that they are worthy of our trust or we outsource the trustworthiness ratings to the third-party institutions (e.g., gossiping, credit ratings, etc.).

Finally, there's more to human communication than expressions and eye gaze. We are also highly verbal communicators, and it turns out that we are also capable of recognizing emotions from the intonation in speech. This skill draws on a set of various structures, some of which are also implicated in the visual recognition of emotions: upon hearing the emotional stimulus, the brain simulates the physiological state associated with that emotion. As a result, the emotion is "felt" in the body. (For a more technical treatment, see Adolphs, Damasio, and Tranel, 2002).

Social exchange reasoning

Gigerenzer (2002) proposed that our ability to pick out such subtle social cues and act on them could be explained with the pre-existence of what he calls triggering algorithms. Upon being triggered, these algorithms activate the necessary modules in the brain called for by the circumstances. Imagine we sense a movement in the dark. Our brain's first reaction will be deciding if the object is animate or inanimate based on the motion patterns. If the object appears to be self-propelled, the triggering algorithm will probably set us into a state of physiological and emotional arousal, followed by behavioral routines like stopping and preparing our body for a fast acceleration, etc., in case we need to flee from a dangerous creature. Similarly, in social situations, triggering algorithms help us decipher whether statements of the form, "If you x, then I'll y," ought to be perceived as threats or as social contracts by activating, among other things, the emotions appropriate for the situation.

Take the following statements:

If you are going to be exposed to a loud sound, you must wear earplugs.
If you clean the dishes, you will be allowed to take a cookie from the jar.

These both are permission rules as well as logical conditional statements. The first statement is a precautionary rule while the latter is a more typical example of a social contract. Fiddick (2004) found that the presence of a benefit (which is the case with all social contracts) predicts inferences about emotional reactions people might have to seeing someone violate a permission rule (e.g., not taking the precaution, or taking the cookie without cleaning): social contract violations are thought to trigger anger, whereas precautionary violations are thought to trigger fear. Although both statements follow the same pattern of conditional logic, they seem to be processed differently and tend to evoke different emotional reactions. I will deal with emotions more thoroughly in Chapter 4.

Up until now, I have been trying—hopefully successfully—to show you that we, as humans, are very skilled at processing (often effortlessly) socially relevant information, thanks to our long history as a species of social exchange. Our highly specialized brains are uniquely adapted to help us navigate social circumstances to help us have larger communities, more effective pair bonds, and recognize potentially trustworthy partners. In other words, our brains are highly effective in helping us foster positive social connections. But how is it at solving the problem of avoiding negative connections? Can it help us, for example, detect cheaters?"

What is a cheater? It is the party that violates the social contract by failing to reciprocate. Perhaps a contractor who does not deliver despite the fact that he has been paid is a perfect case in point. Given the ubiquity of the social norms that regulate our daily interactions, as a species, we have to be hard-wired to detect free-riding (or norm violations in general). In other words, as evolutionary game theorists would put it, our naiveté when it comes to identifying cheaters (i.e., those who fail to reciprocate) would not have been an evolutionarily stable strategy given the negative fitness consequences of possessing such a trait. As mentioned earlier, cheater detection could be considered a sign of a cognitive specialization for social exchange rather than a special case of a context-independent overall intelligence. But can we ever prove that? A clever way to test whether we have such domain-specific cognitive specialization is to see if our brain processes conditional reasoning differently as the context changes from the domain of pure logic to that of a social setting. Since all social contracts are conditional ("If you satisfy x's requirement, then you will be able to receive a benefit from x"), it fits the template of the Wason selection test, a common tool for investigating conditional reasoning (see Wason (1968) for more on this task).

Consider the following argument: if a person sleeps less than five hours, he will have red eyes the next morning. Your objective is to find a way to prove this statement false, but you must not use more information than absolutely necessary. You are provided with four two-sided cards, each of which represents one person. One side of the card tells you if the person slept less than five hours; the other side, whether the person has red eyes. The four cards are shown below. In an attempt to disprove the above statement, which four cards do you flip over? Remember, do not use more information than necessary (i.e., only turn over the minimum number of cards necessary; no shot gunning allowed).

1: Slept less than 5 hours
2: Slept more than 5 hours
3: Has red eyes
4: Does not have red eyes

Now consider the following argument: if a person borrows a friend's car, she should return the car with the tank full.

Again, using the minimum amount of information, you must prove whether this rule has been violated—that is, whether someone has cheated). Again, you are provided with four cards, each one representing a separate case. One side tells you if the person has borrowed the car; the other side, whether the person filled up the tank. Which four cards do you flip to test whether the rule has been violated?

1: Borrowed the car
2: Did not borrow the car
3: Filled up the tank with gas
4: Did not fill up the tank with gas

The answer is the same in both problems: the first and the fourth card should be flipped. The success rate, however, varies drastically between these questions. Why is this the case? After all, they are logically identical in their construction. Cosmides and Tooby (2015) provide a compelling answer:

> Does this result generalize to conditional rules that express a social contract? No. People, who ordinarily cannot detect violations of if-then rules, can do so easily and accurately when that violation represents cheating in a situation of social exchange. This pattern—good violation detection for social contracts but not for descriptive rules—is dissociation in reasoning elicited by differences in the conditional rule's content. It provides (initial) evidence that the mind has reasoning procedures specialized for detecting cheaters (p. 596).

Cooperative mind

Without the elements of our social intelligence outlined so far, human cooperation would have remained much more primitive. We show signs of the fairly elaborate skills required to recognize, engage in, and remain mutually committed to joint activities as soon as we turn three (Gräfenhain et al., 2009). Tomasello and Carpenter (2007), in a series of remarkable experiments done with children, observed that even one-year olds share goals and plans while playing. Even more interestingly, they seem to enjoy collaborative activity more than the instrumental goal compared to primates that are much more goal-oriented. Such collaboration is a characteristic and important trait of us as a species.

There are many universal social behaviors that would indicate that we possess species-specific intelligence despite of their cultural variations. Consider our unique ability to coordinate our efforts and engage in joint efforts on a scale no other species has matched. Coordination requires a set of rules, which could be abstract or more tangible. They also may be context-specific—that is, applicable only under special contexts. Fiske and Haslam (2005) proposed four fundamental principles (that can sometimes occur in combination) that guide our cooperation in various contexts: communal sharing (CS), authority ranking (AR), equality matching (EM), and market pricing (MP). For instance, in completing a task, the group members could simply pitch in without being instructed what to do (CS); they could instead be given orders (AR); each one could take on equal amount of work (EM); or members could decide their amount of contribution contingent upon the understanding that their share will be commensurate with their contribution (MP). These same categories are also used for distributional justice considerations. We would expect any social rule guided by CS to be more sensitive to the differential needs of the individual group members. AR assigns to the person in a position of authority (e.g., elderly) a greater say in the distribution of resources. EM prescribes equal shares as morally justifiable. MP leaves the distribution to be determined by utilitarian principles of merit.

Depending on the context, a certain principle (or a set of them) becomes the operating norm others would be inappropriate for that particular setting. For instance, nobody would suggest that a birthday cake be distributed based on merit. The specific implementation of these four universal principles highlights cultural distinctions, leading to unique patterns of cooperation. Consider arranged marriages, wherein the elders who hold the authority choose their children's partners. This is common in some cultures but simply unthinkable in others in which marriages symbolize mutual affection. Similarly, Moose of Burkina Faso would not consider land as a commodity to be exchanged, even though land is valued for its investment properties in other cultures. We are continually reminded of the existence of these categories when they collide in the struggle to assign monetary value to items acquired outside a market transaction, such as a wedding ring. We even engage in mental accounting to separate these realms, for instance, by treating $10 gained as a windfall differently than $10 received from the grandma for our birthday.

These principles, capable of generating micro-scale social orders in various realms (e.g., family, tribe, etc.), can be scaled up. When we examine the evolution of human societies, as outlined by Johnson and Earle (2006) and Polanyi (2001), we can identify periods where each specific mode of cooperation was dominant, from the more communitarian and reciprocal organization of the hunter-gatherers to the more hierarchical organization of chiefdoms. From this point of view, the market system emerges as a form of economic integration with its own supporting set of institutions.

The rest of this book will further address these "soft skills" that are innate to human psychology and draw on many common physiological resources in the human body. There are five such skills, without which, I believe, the market exchange would not have reached the prominent position it has today: (1) feeling, communicating, and recognizing positive and negative social emotions (e.g., shame); (2) having finely-tuned reciprocal behavioral algorithms (e.g., trust); (3) being able to mentalize (e.g., empathy); (4) being able to exercise self-control (e.g., override the temptation associated with immediate gratification); and (5) having the potential to imitate and conform. Before engaging in a closer inspection of the biological origins of such skills, I would like to highlight the inadequacy of the way in which human motivation has been treated in economics. I will draw on the most recent scientific evidence and evolutionary theorizing to suggest a general and more plausible model that will inform the subsequent chapters.

Part II

Economizing brain

3 Cognitively lazy

Jeremy Bentham once said, "A thing is said to promote the interest, or to be for the interest, of an individual, when it tends to add to the sum total of his pleasures: or, what comes to the same thing, to diminish the sum total of his pains" (2018, p. 2). Although succinct, I believe this statement describes human motivation fairly well. We seek things that are pleasurable and avoid things that are painful, whether consciously or not. One could even argue that it's, to a degree, self-evident; nonetheless, I would like to present a much more nuanced version.

Benthamite utilitarianism—the above view that things hold value inasmuch as they increase pleasure or diminish pain—has constituted the core of mainstream economic theories of human motivation and the official ethical stance in economic policy discussions—a stance disguised behind a veil of common sense. Economists have been generally served well by adopting Bentham's conception of the governing dynamics behind what we do; however, economic applications of Bentham's initial insights have been far too narrow to be considered a comprehensive theory of human motivation. Take Gregory Mankiw's widely read textbook, *Principles of Economics* (2015). The book opens with a list of the ten principles in economics, one of which is the following: "People respond to incentives[1]." Again, this seems self-evident. Or is it? Upon closer inspection, the principle strikes me as one without much substance; basically, it is equivalent to saying, to borrow a line from the PhD comedian Yoram Bauman, "People are motivated by motives." No other market exchange behavior reflects the complexity of human motivation as effectively as does tipping behavior at restaurants. A typical economic explanation, along the people-respond-to-incentives approach, would be that the tip is a response to the service performance or quality in frequented establishments. However, this explanation barely scratches the surface. Avoidance of guilt, gaining social approval, obtaining status, and treating others equitably are among the possible (and perhaps more dominant) motivations behind this complex behavior (Lynn, 2015).

Arrow (1986) once said, "But as far as individual behavior is concerned, any coherent theory of reactions to the stimuli appropriate in an economic context (prices in the simplest case) could in principle lead to a theory of the economy" (p. 386). He was right, in principle. A theory, for instance, that predicts that we buy more of an item as it gets cheaper (all else remaining the same) is indeed a good theory. However, the same theory hits a wall when prices are reduced to zero dollars, making them free. This happens because the theory fails to consider the conditions under which social norms become dominant in guiding behavior such that the typical cost-benefit analysis (i.e., maximize pleasure per dollar spent) simply fades away (Ariely, Gneezy, & Ernan, 2018).

A theory that explains human economic decisions as being based on a rational calculation of costs and benefits may sound intuitive—or at least enticing—because we would like to believe that we are in full control of our own decisions; however, such a theory would be helpless in explaining why positively or negatively worded messages, although communicating similar information, may be perceived differently from one another. For instance, in order to discourage visitors not to take petrified wood from a national park, a group of researchers found that the most effective communication strategy is to notify the visitors that theft is "strongly disapproved," whereas a sign that simply communicates that theft is "regrettably frequent" is not only ineffective but also counter-productive (Cialdini et al., 2006). Such experiments are not mere word games. On the contrary, they cleverly demonstrate the complexity of human motivation and its susceptibility to various subtle influences most likely processed by context-specific emotional systems and by our selective attention to particular social cues in the environment.

Rationality revisited, the nth time

I feel that there is enough said about the inadequacy of the treatment of human behavior in economics. I will not dwell on this subject extensively except referring you to a few notable criticisms from within the field. For instance, Vernon Smith has delivered one of the strongest intellectual critiques from within the field of constructivist rationality, which has been the official behavioral theory in economics. He argued that our brains are built to conserve attentional, conceptual, and symbolic thought resources because these resources are not abundant. Therefore, our brains delegate most decision-making to autonomic processes, including affect and emotive responses that operate without our conscious attention. This economizing property of the brain is our strength, not our weakness, as one may be tempted to assume. The brain's power to "automatize" (Camerer, Loewenstein, and Prelec, 2004) is responsible for our mastery in tasks that seem daunting at first, such driving. With enough practice, our economizing brain gradually succeeds in reducing its demand on cognitive effort—a resource that is extremely scarce and extremely precious.

Similarly, Herbert Simon (1955) much earlier warned us about the misguided belief that economists tend to hold about our computational capacities and the "severe demands" they impose on the decision-makers. He went on to suggest that we, as boundedly rational individuals, often insert simplifications into our model of the world in complex choice situations, such as pricing our house. Simon was certainly onto something. Our species must be smart enough to adapt, within its biological limitations, to the informational complexities present in our environment. Our economizing brain appears to be very well suited for this goal. We naturally develop rules of thumb, and they are effective when followed in the appropriate setting, even in spite of their apparent ignorance and simplicity. Gigerenzer and Goldstein (1996) offered one of the most brilliant demonstrations that substantiates Simon's position. They found that the "Take The Best" (a form of satisficing) algorithm, which relies on a single most-discriminating cue (e.g., name recognition) rather than integrating all the existing cues, draws as many—if not more—correct inferences about unknown features of a real-world environment as any of the more rational, integration algorithms. In other words, our brain is capable of turning its computational shortcomings into major strengths.

A brain that is on autopilot until it is not

> Airbus tends to rely more heavily on automation, giving the computer control unless the pilot overrides it. Boeing favors letting the human make the final decision with automated systems guiding and assisting, but not dictating. (Jack Stewart, 2017)

The automatic versus reflective distinction has found its most elaborate treatment in Daniel Kahneman's (2013) recent book, Thinking Fast and Thinking Slow. System 1, the term he uses to describe the automatic system in the brain, is the repository of various rules of thumb (or heuristics, as they are often called in behavioral economics) and guides much of our daily behavior. In fact, these psychological biases that behavioral economics has devoted itself to studying, are at the core of the systematic errors we make and are driven by a mismatch between our modern environment and the environment in which System 1 evolved and to which it is adapted (most likely a hunter-gatherer lifestyle in the Pleistocene). Dan Sperber's (1985) distinction between dispositions and susceptibilities offers a very useful vocabulary to make sense of this mismatch. We can think of dispositions as adaptive in the environment in which they were originally developed, such as our sweet tooth: although we are disposed to eat sweet food, which, because of its high caloric content and easy digestibility, was an important commodity to our ancestors, in our modern environment, where sugar can be artificially and easily produced and consumed, this disposition results in a susceptibility to over-consumption of sugar at the expense of our long-term health. Many of our ancient dispositions, needless to say, tend to become susceptibilities today. What makes Thaler and Sunstein's "nudges" a highly effective behavioral intervention is the fact that they bypass System 2 and directly target tendencies within the automatic brain and, as a result, manipulates behavior unconsciously, thereby bypassing conscious thinking, which is, as we all know so well, quite effortful.

In economics, a similar distinction between automatic and controlled processes is offered by Camerer, Loewenstein, and Prelec (2005) in a seminal piece that sought to bring economics into conversation with neuroscience, launching a new field: neuroeconomics. Automatic processes, by definition, are performed effortlessly and are not accessible to consciousness while they are operating. They are the default mode of our brain's operation and may be interrupted when, for instance, something novel pops up in the environment. This understanding is analogous to Airbus' approach to automation in planes. Or, for a more relatable example, imagine you find out that the road you take to work every day is closed for traffic. When you take notice, thanks to emotional feedback (e.g., a startle sensation), you consider alternative routes and evaluate them in terms of distance and other important factors. Bravo! Your brain just successfully switched to its controlled mode.

Camerer et al. make another interesting observation as to the interaction between the automatic and controlled processes: when we are guided by our automatic system (e.g., procrastinating), we feel a powerful drive to make sense of our own behavior even though we do not have conscious access to the processes driving them. As a result, we attribute behavior to our deliberative (i.e., conscious) decision processes and construct narratives to that explain our behaviors. Apparently, *Homo sapiens* is more of a rationalizing animal than a rational one (Lo, 2017).

Neuroscientifically, we more or less can trace automatic and controlled processes to the brain regions where they originate. For instance, the amygdala, buried below the cortex, is responsible for automatic affective responses such as fear. On the other hand, the orbital and pre-frontal cortex are in command of the controlled processes that we engage in deliberately. Therefore, it is a fitting description that we sometimes call the pre-frontal cortex (where the System 2 resides) the "executive brain:" it receives inputs from various regions, integrates them, and translates them into goals to be executed.

This dual-process model creates an image of the brain that consists of a hierarchical organization wherein System 1 recommends and System 2 adopts (or vetoes). This means, as Andrew Lo explains, that when it comes to guiding our actions, one component of the brain can override another under certain specialized conditions. For instance, our swiftly instinctive fear reactions via the amygdala—the "quick and dirty route," as LeDoux (1996) calls it—can dominate the higher brain functions of the prefrontal cortex under sufficiently threatening circumstances. Imagine you hear a loud noise that sounds like a gunshot. While your executive brain is probably trying to keep you calm by telling you that it was just an exhaust backfire, your amygdala guides you to duck and look for cover quickly. Despite its simplicity (or perhaps because of it), this model is quite useful.

A series of evidence from the field of affective neuroscience, led by Panksepp's experiments with various mammalian species, suggests some form of hierarchical organization between the subcortical regions, where the primary affects such as anger are instantiated, and the cortex, which works to inhibit and/or regulate emotions (Liotti & Panksepp, 2004). Activation in the anterior insula in reaction to unfair offers in ultimatum games is a good predictor of rejection rates (Sanfey et al., 2003); however, when that activation is accompanied by activation in the dorsolateral prefrontal cortex (an area implicated in goal maintenance and executive control), the negative emotions associated with the unfair offers seem to be modified and rejection rates are reduced (Miller and Cohen, 2001). One plausible interpretation is that a higher cognitive effort may be required to overcome the strong emotional tendency to reject low offers in order to accomplish the overall goal of gaining as much as possible (Kenning and Plassmann, 2005). (More on cognitive control is discussed in Chapter 7.)

"Affect" heuristic: "If it feels good, it must be good."

The automatic system goes by many different—and appropriately descriptive—names, such as gut feelings (Gigerenzer) and folk intuitions (Steven Pinker). It motivates an array of behavioral responses effortlessly through a set of processes, many of which may not reach the threshold of awareness. It draws on various brain regions, nervous systems throughout the body, neurotransmitters, the endocrine system, etc., and serves many specialized purposes. These gut feelings originate, as expected, in the evolutionarily older sections of the brain, are shared by other animals, and are successful at singling out simple but relevant cues in our environment. A tacit (i.e., non-learned) skill of this system, one that we count on in our social relations, would be our inner intuitive economist. We have the natural ability to engage in reciprocal exchange thanks to our intuitive favor-accounting ability—the basis of many of our spontaneously emerged institutions codified effectively by the phrase in Hammurabi's code, "An eye for an eye, and a tooth for a tooth."

The reason why the automatic system is associated with gut feelings or intuitions is no accident. First of all, there is indeed a robust interaction between the enteric nervous system (i.e., nerves of the gut) and the central nervous system (i.e., brain and spinal cord). More importantly, the automatic system owes its efficiency to what Slovic and his colleagues (2007) aptly call the "affect heuristics." Simply put, affect helps us rate emotional stimuli using a binary coding system for how it makes us feel: good or bad. This evaluation of the valence of the emotions is always very quick, but may not always be conscious. Affect, this way, has a direct and primary role in motivating behavior. When we face an event of emotional significance, our brain naturally searches for the emotion associated with that event. Depending on the activated feelings, either pleasant or unpleasant, we engage in or avoid an action based on whether it will reproduce that feeling (pleasant) or reduce it (unpleasant). Because the affective system is pleasure-pain oriented, it processes the stimuli rapidly and is not burdened by logical justification. Instead, it follows the simple rule, "if it feels good, it must be good."

One of the major misconceptions about the role of affect and emotions is that they are always opposed to logic, resulting in the commonly held emotion versus reason dichotomy. Admittedly, this distinction may have some neural basis. It is also true the brain has some properties of a hierarchal organization. However, a much more plausible approach, one that is also in line with recent experimental evidence that will be discussed more extensively in the next chapter, would be the following: it is unlikely that we can employ any rational thinking at all without at least some guidance from affect somewhere along the line. Thus, it is not too farfetched to assume that our ability to experience feelings that are linked to biological regulation must have been prerequisite for developing effective reasoning faculties. Most of our "thoughts" take the form of rough images and narratives that originate in the affective system (Damasio, 2017). These images are tagged with positive or negative feelings of varying degrees. These readily available affective impressions provide us with many mental short-cuts and help us economize the cognitive resources that are scarce.

In the absence of affect, we probably would feel as though we are getting bombarded with mountains of stimuli that have little to no information value. This is evident in situations where the stimuli do not lend themselves to any meaningful affective representation. For instance, we find it rather difficult to determine our willingness of pay for an item if it is relatively novel and presented to us in isolation with no other options to which it can be compared. Imagine two separate groups of individuals are asked to evaluate the following options independently:

	Dictionary A	*Dictionary B*
Year of publication:	1993	1993
Number of entries:	10,000	20,000
Any defects?	No, it's like new.	Yes, the cover's torn Otherwise it's like new.

When these options are evaluated in isolation, Dictionary A was rated much more highly, even though it is clearly inferior with regards to the more important attribute (i.e., number of entries); however, when both options are present, the preferences are reversed (Hsee, 1996). Apparently, certain types of attributes are much more difficult to evaluate independently than others. The value of the number of entries cannot be mapped into an affective impression easily, yet the condition of the cover can. That is, we are not sure if the 10,000 entries are good, but the torn cover is certainly bad.

Although the automatic system is the primary form of reasoning for humans, social behavior, as indicated above, is most likely the co-product of these two systems and how they work together. This enables our social behavior to be quick and effective yet retain its flexibility and context-dependent nature (Bohl & van den Bos, 2012). For instance, the mirror system that enables us to simulate somebody else's action (e.g., he is counting the money I just gave him) is supported by a set of low-level automatic processes, while the theory of mind that enables us to guess other people's intentions (e.g., he must not be trusting me) is supported higher-level reflective processes. Both of these systems, and the underlying processes then enable them, help us predict behavior and facilitate social interactions.

Homeostasis-driven preferences: upgrading to Bentham 2.0

When a bear took a dip in a swimming pool in an LA neighborhood on a scorching afternoon in July 2018, an information officer from US Department of Fish and Wildlife described the incident in the following terms: "This is not […] an aggressive bear. We believe the bear was seeking relief from the heat." How was she able to empathize with the bear? After all, swimming pools are not among the cultural inventions of the bear for cooling off. Yet we can easily put ourselves in the bear's shoes because we share many of the same biological needs, including homeostatic thermoregulation (i.e., keeping our body temperature within a comfortable range conducive for normal functioning). The bear's instinct to regulate his body temperature became newsworthy when a homeostatic imbalance led him to act in ways that were deemed unconventional. The public reaction would have been the same, I guess, if you were caught scratching your back by aggressively rubbing it against a tree at a crowded park. We invented back scratchers for a reason.

One of the clearest manifestations of the automatic system is homeostasis, our ability to continuously maintain various physiological variables within a range of values conducive for survival—even for flourishing. Automated homeostatic control is mostly reliable and extremely efficient. Homeostatic processes pertaining to the body's internal environment, such as how dehydration causes the kidneys to slow down their operation, may not produce any observable behavioral reactions. Other homeostatic imperatives can motivate various behavioral reactions, either through non-conscious affective states or, if the disruption of homeostasis is significant, using the feelings as an interface (e.g., covering yourself with blanket when shivering and feeling ill in order to improve your body's immune response by keeping body temperature high). This is the realm where we also observe cultural variations.

Damasio and Damasio (2016) provides the most compelling case when it comes to articulating the centrality of homeostasis to human motivation that is behind many of our (economic and other) actions. I rely on his account through most of this book, whether directly or indirectly. Feelings, he argues, communicate information to our minds as to whether the current state of our body is generally conducive to continued health—or, again, even flourishing. If I were to offer one possible reformulation of Benthamite utilitarianism, it would take the following form: pleasure and pain are feelings that originate in homeostatic mechanisms whose primary function is to detect departures from an ideal range (i.e., in the self's best interest). They also constitute the motivation to restore the equilibrium (Camerer, Loewenstein, & Prelec, 2004).

Our ability to correctly interpret the content, intensity, and valence of our feelings is, therefore, key to deliberately reacting in ways compatible with this homeostatic imperative. Take the feeling of hunger driven by a drop in the level of circulating blood glucose. It motivates a search behavior for possible energy sources. Fat and sugar are immediately pleasurable as they are effective in meeting this goal of securing energy. Translating this into econspeak, we have developed biological preferences for fats and sugars because they promise high utility. Thus, the conscious feelings originating from homeostatic imbalances provide us with a menu of options to choose from to eliminate these imbalances. It may be the change in blood sugar level that triggers hunger, but we are the ones who decide to alleviate it by reaching for the doughnut. This adaptability, needless to say, comes at a cost: some of options may prove to be maladaptive, as in the case of obesity, resulting from overconsumption of sugary treats.

We crave fatty and sweet foodstuffs for another intriguing reason: they are easy to digest. There is a strong signaling mechanism from the gut to the brain, via our nervous system, that provides this input—again without our awareness. But this signaling is not limited to the nervous system. Animal research increasingly points to a connection to the microbiome (the body's microbial community). For instance, Sgritta et al. (2019) and his colleagues found that ASD-related social dysfunction in mice might be able to be improved with injection of a bacteria species knows as Lactobacillus reuteri. In a recent study, Nguyen and her colleges (2018) investigated whether the composition of bacteria in our gut might correlate with the existence of some psychiatric disorders. Among others, they found that Proteobacteria levels were lower in subjects with schizophrenia compared to normal controls. It is too early to tell whether or not our body's microbiome composition could be connected any specific set of behavioral dispositions/pathologies as their primary cause, but it is a compelling explanatory avenue to pursue.

A model that explains human motivation in terms of our body's physiological desire to keep functioning normally and avoid harm is extremely useful. Once understood along these lines, the term "preferences" takes on a more substantive meaning. First and foremost, this framework highlights the transitory nature of our preferences: when our core body temperature is too high, anything that lowers it (e.g., turning on the fan) would feel good, but might stop feeling good once we are at a comfortable temperature. This means that, in many cases, preferences depend on the body's internal state, which provides information signals that initiate actions aimed at achieving a tolerable balance. Many of these actions are executed without us even being aware of them. Or, if we do happen to be aware, we give very little thought to them.

Our psychology has adapted to survive in widely diverse terrestrial environments, all of which have one thing in common: the presence of our conspecifics (i.e., other people). So, it is natural to expect that an absence of the social contact necessary for normal functioning (i.e., proximity) would generate physiological responses in our body similar to other homeostatic imbalances. This, in turn, would activate the "seeking" system (in the sense Panksepp uses the term) that helps us get to much-needed social resources. This desire is driven by the design of the human brain, which assumes that it operates within a relatively predictable social network characterized by familiarity, joint attention, shared goals, and mutual dependence. These conditions make up, as Beckes and Coan (2011) call it, our brain's social baseline, which, as with other homeostatic baselines, we are motivated to maintain. They argue that our inherent desire to form social relations is reflective of our brain's energy-efficient nature: individuals, when they deal with their environmental challenges alone (e.g., sustaining vigilance for potential threats), are forced to engage in effortful executive functions (i.e., prefrontal activity) that can quickly deplete the finite cognitive resources. When we are exposed to a cue that signals possible threats, Coan et al. (2006) found, our brain's response is significantly reduced if we are in the company of a trusted partner as opposed to facing the same situation alone. One plausible explanation for this result is that socially mediated forms of emotion regulation (having a partner present) simply reduce the need for any affective response. Thus, maintaining a social baseline tends to conserve not only the gas, but the brake as well, Beckes and Coan argued. That is, social proximity helps save neural (and, perhaps, peripheral physiological) resources. Our instinctive desire to maintain a social baseline makes the world much more manageable for ourselves and frees up the much-needed resources for higher-level thinking.

In the next chapter, I will articulate the role of emotions behind our social intelligence, building on the view of affect presented in this chapter and showing that emotions are our biggest guardians. They not only serve self-preservational goals, but also help us maintain effective cooperation.

Note

1 His show is available at the following link: https://youtu.be/VVp8UGjECt4.

4 Emotionally smart

> Herbert Simon: "In order to have anything like a complete theory of human rationality, we have to understand what role emotion plays in it" (1983, p. 29).

What are emotions? Why do we have or need them? I argue here that the role of emotions is similar to a theory in the sense that all observations are theory-driven. Empirical observations will not sort themselves out or organize themselves into meaningful patterns without help from some theoretical goggles. While I am sitting in a coffee shop writing these words, my ears are awash with various auditory stimuli, nearly all of which my brain ignores, as they do not communicate any valuable information. This would have changed, I suppose, if I suddenly heard a loud bang. Similarly, our emotions help us filter out unimportant environmental stimuli—a mechanism without which we would be overwhelmed. That is, emotions limit the range of information that we (or any organisms) will consider (Gordon & de Sousa, 1991). Furthermore, not counting isolated, contrived settings like solving math problems, environmental stimuli become intelligible to us only to the extent that our brain/body can translate them into emotional signals. In this sense, it is useful to treat emotions as internally-generated information signals that help focus our attention to specific parameters or aspects of the stimuli; without this focus, we would be paralyzed. Therefore, emotions constitute the core of our intelligence as species:

> By restricting the range of options considered (reducing the load on short and long-term memory), by focusing on certain variables (certain stimuli receive higher ranking order), and by initiating and terminating the evaluation process (working as a satisficing mechanism), emotions supplement the insufficiencies of reason (Hanoch, 2002, p. 7).

When the leading economic journals occasionally publish pieces on the role of emotions in decision making, emotions are usually treated (with

Loewenstein being a major exception) as mal-adaptations that constrain optimal decisions (see Cohen, 2005, for a typical treatment of emotions in economics). Another way in which emotions feature in economic analyses is as non-pecuniary costs (to be avoided) or benefits (to be sought). For instance, we may choose to cross the street (a costly behavior) to avoid coming face to face with a beggar whose visible misery would induce the unpleasant feeling of guilt and thereby subtract from our pleasure. The only relevant aspect of the emotions in this case becomes their valence—their ability to generate subjective pleasure and pain (Elster, 1998). By ignoring the evolutionarily adaptive function of emotions, economists effectively ignore what makes us ecologically rational—a pre-requisite to our survival as a species.

Although environmental circumstances have changed, cognition is still as expensive in terms of the resources it needs, such as time and energy, as it was 500,000 years ago. So, it is not surprising that the neocortex, pressured to economize, would distribute many routine but vital functions, such as attention, to the processes that operate beneath the surface of awareness. By design, we must solve many routine problems by relying on the intelligence embodied in our emotions that are programmed to restore and sustain homeostasis. Moreover, the trade-off between speed and accuracy, discussed earlier in reference to the automatic system, is also true for emotions. Although a rational decision (e.g., calculating probabilities, etc.) might eventually bring about the best outcome, emotions are instrumental for finding good-enough solutions very quickly. They do so by singling-out the most relevant cue in the environment, which in turn activates the emotional mechanism, leading to the appropriate reaction. As LeDoux (1996) exemplified perfectly, if you were a meek prey faced with a vicious predator, if you chose to evaluate the likelihood of each possible choice leading to success or failure, you would end up getting so bogged down in decision making that you would be eaten before you made the choice. Thus, fatal paralysis is the likely outcome of extensive deliberation. Therefore, at the most basic level, emotional responses help us make decisions in situations in which procrastination does not serve our interests.

Motivation

As a field devoted to the study of human behavior, economics has surprisingly little to say about motivation beyond that "we prefer more to less." This is less surprising, however, when you consider that economics lacks the vocabulary to deal with the complexity of motivation. If motivation refers to the forces that cause any organism to initiate and persist in certain behaviors, but not others, we can see that, without emotions, there is simply no motivation. As Shackle (1972) points out, on its own, our calculating brain has no force. Pure reason, on its own, is not capable of animating us or initiating purposeful behavior.

As I mentioned earlier, the tendency to underestimate the centrality of visceral factors to our functioning is partly fueled by the fact that we have conscious access to only some of our emotional experiences. Furthermore, the fact that we, as rationalizing[1] animals, can exercise introspection leads us to exaggerate the significance of higher-order cognitive processes in our behavior (Loewenstein, 2000). A reliable body of the current experimental evidence highlights how common and reliable this over-attribution problem is.

The most convincing pieces of evidence for the centrality of emotions come from the experiments Damasio conducted earlier in his career with emotionally-impaired individuals (due to trauma, etc.) whose other mental faculties remained generally intact. One element that seems to be common for such individuals was that their lives were falling apart. Even though they performed well on any test measuring their intelligence and critical thinking abilities, outside the lab they were prone to repeatedly make bad decisions. At other times, they found themselves in a state of paralysis where they could not decide at all. Their inability to feel emotions had diminished their capacity for reasoning—a process whereby we identify alternatives, imagine outcomes, and determine which alternative is most likely to yield the best outcome.

Emotions help us set our priorities among competing motivated behaviors by providing us with quick estimates of likely consequences of each behavioral option by assigning them pleasure/pain values. While vetting each possible behavioral strategy by simulating it in our minds, each option evokes a particular emotional response or a gut feeling that Damasio calls a somatic marker. We can model this process as an *if-then* search. Consider the following scenario. Imagine that you are contemplating whether you should get dessert after a meal. You first mentally simulate the pleasure you'd derive from satisfying your sweet tooth. Then you remember that you have been trying to be calorie conscious and that ran 3 miles earlier to burn 300 calories. Getting dessert effectively wipes out those entire hard-earned calorie points. You would feel regret and guilt and would experience all the bodily reactions that go along with those emotions. Depending on the strength of each emotion being evoked, you would land on a decision. Ideally, the search ends once you find the behavioral option with the most pleasing (or the least painful) projected emotional outcome. If self-control is strength of yours, you are likely to imagine more *if-then* scenarios (rather than stop at the first) as Bernard et al. (2005) pointed out. The stronger the willpower, the more skilled one becomes at assessing the relative strengths of the emotional responses associated with each option. Thus, emotions serve as a form of valuation system that helps to prevent the type of decision paralysis Damasio's subjects experienced.

Regret and disappointment are two distinctive emotions that are of particular interest to economists, since they are directly tied to the decisions we make (Zeelenberg & Pieters, 2007). Although they are similar, these two emotions tend to motivate different reactions. Regret is the product of counterfactual reasoning and can lead to self-criticism, which in turn motivates a desire to undo the event associated with the emotion. Disappointment, on the other hand, may simply generate a sense of powerlessness without necessarily motivating us to engage in any particular action. Given that the primary function of our emotion system is generate the motivation to engage in goal-directed behavior, since these emotions serve different primary motivational functions, it is expected that they would lead to different behavioral outcomes. Take a consumer who has a negative experience with a service provider (e.g., a cable guy who never showed up); her reaction will be determined by the nature of her emotions she felt as a result of this interaction. If she feels disappointment, she may choose to talk to her friends and seek comfort about the experience. If, on the other hand, she feels regret, it might lead her to re-evaluate her commitment to the service provider (assuming that there are potential alternatives), because regret assigns the responsibility for the negative outcome to ourselves (therefore, she would feel responsible for taking action to change the circumstances).

But this is not mere conjecture about our cognitive processes; there is neuroanatomical evidence supporting the workings of regret. Because regret generates an unpleasant feeling, we are motivated to minimize the frequency with which we experience it. Experiencing regret tends to increase the degree to which we anticipate regret, which, in turn, changes the choice-related activity in our brain: enhanced activity in the right dorsolateral prefrontal (DLPFC), right lateral OFC, and inferior parietal lobule (Coricelli et al., 2005). The fact that the amount of activity observed in the lateral OFC is clearly tied to the level of regret—which corresponded to the difference between the result of the choice made and that of the alternative outcome—indicates the decisions that might result in regret are evaluated differently than disappointment.

In sum, emotions are effective tools for guiding and motivating our decisions and behaviors, helping to save us from decision paralysis. As such, they would have provided a fitness benefit to our ancestors, one that carries over into today's day and age.

Motives

We use the term *motive* to refer to the desires that grab our attention and move us to engage in action. In this sense, motives are closely linked to motivation. Our repertoire of motives must have served adaptive purposes and have grown over time as our group size and brain size (in particular, the neocortex) expanded. The adaptive function of motives is most evident in reflexive behaviors, such as seeking safety (e.g., recoiling) that are rooted in the older structures of in the brain, namely the brain stem and diencephalon.

Some of our motives, however, are evolutionarily more recent. These motives tend to be domain-sensitive, become activate under the particular social domains for which they were designed. (See Bernard et al., 2005, for a complete set of hierarchical motives.) For instance, the decision to self-sacrifice on a battlefield (one of the strongest forms of altruism) may not emanate from the same set of motives as status-signaling (e.g., conspicuous garments) to attract mates does. Self-sacrifice for non-kin[2] draws on motives that would not exist if we lacked the memetic motives that allow us to create a sense of abstract group membership—that is, a cultural kinship. Status-signaling, on the other hand, is common among most species, although it has reached its most elaborate manifestation with humans. Because they are unique and triggered by different domains, motives could oppose one another in certain circumstances and align in others, interacting to affect our decisions. It is possible that economic choices we make originate simultaneously from a diverse set of motives relevant to different social configurations. For instance, a new gadget (e.g., iPhone X) may serve our curiosity while helping us communicate social status and build cooperative alliances via social media.

Some of our more evolutionarily recent motives are geared toward expanding our cooperation and mutually beneficial interactions beyond the confines of our family. Although affection is the basis for maintaining dyadic relationships and caring for young, its capacity for building cooperative alliances has some limits. Altruistic motives and conscience support the extensive cooperative outcomes in growingly complex social environments. Such motives, like all motives, become intelligible (and then actionable, leading to subsequent motivated behavior) through the core affects (Russell, 2003) they are able generate—the qualitative states felt as good or bad. Rephrasing Bentham's wisdom (again), it is plausible, as a general principle, to think that we seek experiences associated with positively valenced emotions (e.g., care) and avoid those evoking negatively valenced emotions (e.g., guilt). That said, this valence-based approach would come up short in predicting actual behavior (i.e., when multiple options are present, and not just the contrived laboratory situations with binary-choice scenarios) where acting on the emotion-specific concern is the rule. Instead, I argue for an approach to the behavioral consequences of emotions that largely overlaps the feeling-is-for-doing approach offered by Zeelenberg and Pieter (2006), which is more pragmatic in its orientation: "… specific emotions, because of the specific meaning they convey to the decision maker, may help us better understand the goals and motivations of the decision maker …." (p. 128).

I take a particular interest in social emotions (e.g., guilt and shame) here, as they are integral to scaling up human cooperation. Moreover, not only do we need to be able to experience these emotions, but need to be able to recognize them in others for them to be useful information signals. The existence of so-called "emotional contagion" (i.e., our ability to catch emotions from others) attests to how sensitive and in tune we are with the emoting faces, gestures, postures, etc., surrounding us (Goleman, 2005). For instance, altruistic behavior relies on our enhanced sensitivity to the fear and vulnerability of others. Our species owes its ability to engage in sophisticated forms of social exchange to its ability to feel (and, to a certain extent, manipulate) social emotions.

Social feelings

One might expect emotions (or "passions" as enlightenment scholars used to call them) to promote anti-social behavior, as they are sensitive to the immediacy of the reward or pain. After all, social relations need to be nurtured and are not very tolerant of the opportunistic temptations some emotions provide. Furthermore, primary key function of social norms is to inhibit spontaneous, emotion-driven action tendencies (e.g., a more subdued reaction to a fearsome stimulus). However, in spite of this, our sociality is deeply emotional. Our social intelligence (or rationality, in the ecological sense) is supported by a set of very strong emotional predispositions called social emotions. As DeSteno et al. (2010) put it, "If the ability to act cooperatively in economic exchange, and thereby build trust, is socially adaptive, then it would make sense that specific emotional responses exist to foster it" (p. 289). Thus, it is expected that specific affective states would underlie many forms of economic exchange.

Since we are emotive beings, social exchange inevitably has integral affective components, without which it would not have its elaborate form that we observe today. For cooperative social groups to develop at all—and, even more, to remain cohesive—those who participate in the social exchange must, above all else, associate the group itself (independent of the specific individuals populating it) with some positive feelings. And they do. The frequency of exchange tends to correlate positively with feelings, which in turn lead to cohesion, which promotes commitment.

Lawler and his colleagues (2008) found that in a productive exchange arrangement—one which involves a jointly-produced collective good from which participating individuals benefit, such as a co-authorship relation or a business partnership—strong positive emotions are more likely to be attributed to the social units (rather than to participants themselves) compared to other exchange arrangements like reciprocal trades. This outcome is expected given the greater interdependence and the higher sense of shared responsibility in such relationships. As a result, compared to different exchange arrangements, those who engage in productive exchange feel a greater degree of group solidarity and report the greatest attachment to their group or network. When agents share and jointly pursue goals, which is the case here, it is more likely that they adopt a "we" (or collectively intentional) mode of cooperation that is supported by a unique motivational state (Tuomela, 2007).

Guardians of self-preservation and the collective survival enterprise

Up until now, I have primarily articulated the connection between emotions and motivation from an evolutionary perspective. In this section, building on the principles laid out so far in this chapter, I have two specific points to make regarding the adaptive function of social emotions.

(1) Social emotions motivate cooperative behavior while protecting the individual against exploitation in communal life; and
(2) The extensive market system would not have been achieved if the co-operation was not perceived as valuable (or rewarding) *independent* of its instrumental uses.

One of the most useful demonstrations of the emotive make up our brain is the behavioral pattern of generalized reciprocity. It is a complicated form of social behavior, as the object of the cooperative behavior is usually a complete stranger. For instance, when manipulated to feel grateful, DeSteno and his colleagues (2010) found that we have the tendency to pay the favor forward by acting more cooperatively toward strangers in one-off instances, even when the decision is made in complete privacy (i.e., there is no perceived threat of retaliation). However, generalized reciprocity also has a darker side: the negative emotions associated with unfair treatments could influence our subsequent decision. The study conducted by Strang and her colleagues (2016) reached the conclusion that generalized negative reciprocity may result from a process similar to the primate behavior called "displaced aggression" (de Waal, 2006) that involves multiple hierarchical layers of whipping boys. The participants who feel they received less than their fair share in a dictator game tended to be much less generous to strangers in subsequent rounds where they were in the position of power. Even more interestingly, when the unfairly treated participants were given the chance to vent their feelings by responding the to the malevolent dictator in writing, they acted much less pettily in the next round.

You may consider generalized reciprocity a trivial component of our behavioral repertoire. Yes, your boss yelled at you, and then you yelled at your subordinate, and so on. So what? This is merely indicative of the lingering effects of the emotions, subsequently turning into moods and coloring your appraisal of future events, as is predicted by the appraisal-tendency theory (Lerner & Keltner, 2000). But how about reciprocal altruism, which is, in essence, a form of enlightened self-interest that finds its most advanced expression in the market exchange? Shouldn't it be the realm of cool-headed calculations? (I'll tackle this question in depth in the next chapter.) The evidence shows that, without the psychological evolution of emotions such as guilt, shame, or anger, we would be prone to succumbing to the temptation of short-term opportunism or of being exposed to unfair treatment even in the domain of mutually beneficial trade.

The capacity of the human brain to feel shame, for instance, has been used to develop sophisticated means of inflicting shame on group members (e.g., public nakedness) who misbehave and transgress against their neighbors and friends (Wettlaufer, 2012). Elster's (1998) treatment of shame, although not informed by any evolutionary framework, captures the role of social emotions rather effectively. One of the most significant triggers for feeling shame is the threat of social ostracism. Materials sanctions, such as discontinuing trading with a party, as a punishment for norm violations, would be effective, but not for the reasons economists typically put forward. They are effective to the extent that they are seen as vehicles of the emotion of content (or disgust)—a point captured by Hirschman (1985):

> Economists often propose to deal with unethical or antisocial behavior by raising the cost of that behavior rather than proclaiming standards and imposing prohibitions and sanctions. [...] principal purpose of publicly proclaimed laws and regulations is to stigmatize antisocial behavior and thereby to influence citizens' values and behavior codes (p. 10).

Interestingly, refraining from trading with someone on account of norm violations has consequences not only for the violating party, but also for the party imposing the sanction. Both parties rely on such economic exchanges, but if the offense is significant, the offended party (the one imposing the sanction), may be willing to forgo the benefits of that exchange in order to punish the offender, and the higher the cost the sanctioner is willing to incur, the more strongly it communicates a feeling of contempt: "the costs to the sanctioner are what makes the sanction really painful to the target. It tells him that others see him as so bad that they are willing to forego valuable opportunities rather than have to deal with him" (Elster, 1998, p. 67). Therefore, policies that successfully evoke shame would potentially yield greater compliance with the rules. For example, Coricelli and his colleagues (2010) found that the risk of public exposure of deception may have a greater change of reducing the likelihood of tax evasion than monetary penalties.

Our evolutionary development of emotions, like feeling anger when mistreated, was a prerequisite for our development social relationships that are durable over the long-term. Therefore, emotions motivated—and continue to motivate—the type of behavioral responses that are ecologically rational: they either encourage us to engage in cooperative relationships or protect us after having entered one. Lacking an emotional reaction to, say, an injustice done to you, is equivalent to lacking the situationally appropriate reflexes to duck when somebody swings a fist at you. Therefore, as Pagel (2012) points out, our sense of fairness serves like a police force and watches out for our interest. In this sense, simply returning a favor or repaying betrayal with revenge (a.k.a., tit-for-tat strategy), should come naturally to us and was most likely the winning strategy (i.e., the most effective) in our social interactions in the past. Anger seems to have a similar function. The emotional state of being angry is involuntarily triggered if we are feeling cheated in a social exchange (e.g., wage cuts); its primary purpose is help us feel a negative utility that could be alleviated when we punish the suspected cheater. Therefore, it is not necessarily a weakness, as we commonly assume, but a strength. As Cohen and Dickens (2002) sum up perfectly, "The ability to experience anger becomes functional [...] since it communicates a commitment to punish even in circumstances where punishment is 'suboptimal,' and thus facilitates cooperation."

Robert Axelrod and William Hamilton's well-known contest/experiment (1981) seems to have lent some credibility to this line of reasoning. Evidently, the tit-for-tat strategy proved to be the best one (in terms of payoff) in a repeated Prisoners' Dilemma game. This outcome, as we see it, highlights two behavioral tendencies in humans that are particularly noteworthy for the purposes of this book: (1) the motivation to punish the non-conformist is strong, and (2) there is a cooperative bias as individuals try signaling their cooperative intentions (by cooperating in the first game or after getting penalized) despite the risk of taking a short-term personal loss.

Cooperation feels good

Recent neuro-scientific evidence has further bolstered our convictions that these tendencies are most likely hardwired, and, even more, shows that mutual cooperation in social exchanges has its own reward beyond the monetary gains associated with it. For instance, there is activation in the ventral striatum (the reward/pleasure area of the brain) after a mutually cooperative outcome in Prisoner's Dilemma games, but only when the subject is paired with a human partner (as opposed to a computer), even when controlling for monetary gain (Rilling et al., 2002).

The recent experimental evidence with the ultimatum game (where one party receives a sum of money and offers some of it to their partner) supports the notion that rejection of an offer (which results in no payoff for either party) functions as a signal back to the proposer; after all, it is the only viable social communication mechanism available in these impersonal experimental settings. In one such study, Xiang, Lohrenz, and Montague (2013) found that anterior insula activation predicted the probability of rejecting unfair offers (i.e., offers that fell short of what the receivers expected). Considering the proposed role of the anterior insula in disgust, generating awareness and subjective feelings, and responding to norm violations in social exchange situations, among other things, a felt need to punish unfair behavior is the most plausible explanation for people's actions in this game. Xiao and Houser (2005), in a cleverly modified version of the same experiment, tested whether people can modify their retaliatory motivation to punish large deviations from egalitarian distribution by being allowed to express their feelings before acting. They found that the recipients are less likely to use costly punishment, and instead accept unfair outcomes, if they have a less expensive alternative mechanism to express negative emotions toward the proposers. This supports the notion that rejection functions as a signal to the proposer, one that expresses how the recipient perceives and feels about the offer.

In this light, the rejection of an unfair offer can be seen as a form of altruistic punishment: the punished party does not stand to gain from the punishment in a one-time game, though the punishment will likely benefit the community overall, as it may teach the punished party to play more fairly. This altruistic punishment is commonplace and hardwired. Fehr and Gächter (2002) demonstrated that in public good games, when given the opportunity, there is a strong tendency on the part of the above-average contributors to punish—at their own expense, mind you, as all interactions are one-off—those who contribute less than the average. They trace the source of altruistic punishment to negative emotions such as anger and annoyance associated with free riding behavior, as revealed by the interviews done with the punishers afterwards. Moreover, the motivation to punish uncooperative (anti-social) behavior appears to be stronger than the propensity to reward pro-social behavior, a finding attributed to a corresponding asymmetry in emotional intensity, wherein emotions are more intense when one is treated unfavorably (Offerman, 2002).

Aversion to market

From all of this evidence, I hope it is by now clear that market exchange is not a realm of cool-headed calculations of potential pleasure and pain units—for most of us, anyway. It is a realm of social interactions with real emotional consequences. It is completely natural for us to be suspicious of our potential trade partners because, naturally, we have a strong aversion to getting deceived, exploited, or treated unfairly. What is at stake is much more than potential utility losses that we can simply write off in order to move on with our lives. Emotional consequences of economic exchange are much more substantial and widespread. This idea was captured very well by the following observation made by McFadden (2006) in his presidential address at the 117th meeting of American Economic Association: "trade is part of the way that humans as social animals define and defend themselves, a process that is both cognitive and visceral." When markets do not work well, they are potential sources of frustration and grief, as are many of our social relations.

Another strong motivator that might feed our fear of the market is our aversion to the strong emotional disutility associated with betrayal that goes beyond the financial loss. Betrayal aversion is a strong emotion that probably evolved to keep reciprocation rates high. That said, the institutional backdrop becomes one of the chief determinants of whether our desire to engage in economic exchange outweighs the emotional resistance to see our trust get betrayed. Imagine you are playing a trust game where you (the investor) are given $10 and two options: you can either split it with your partner (the trustee), with each party getting $5—a safe return. Alternatively, you can invest your money with the trustee such that you triple the $10, but with a caveat: there is no guarantee that you would earn more than $5, as it is solely in the trustee's control how to divvy up the return. Would you trust? Would others? It depends. A group of people who participated in this experiment were more willing to entrust their money to their partner if they were shielded from the knowledge of whether they have been betrayed (Aimone and Houser, 2013). Furthermore, the betrayal aversion proved to be so strong that the participants in the trust game tended to be much more comfortable to delegate the post-investment allocations to a computer rather than another person, even though the baseline betrayal probabilities were the same in each case.

This particular reaction should not be surprising and tells us about the selective significance we assign to the difference between intentional and unintentional behavior. For instance, if we are harmed by, say, being given wrong directions unintentionally, we would be much more forgiving than if we were deliberately misled. When Aimone, Houser, and Weber (2014) investigated the brain activity while the participants made their choices, there appeared to be variations in the insula depending on whether the investor was playing a person or the computer. Activation was greatest when trusting another person, less when trusting the computer, and least when playing safe. Considering the role of the insula in generating awareness social exchange situations, this outcome should not be surprising.

Notes

1 Rationalizing may also, as Elster (1998) suggested, be a strategy to ease the pain associated with moral emotions such as guilt, say, after you stole something.

2 Self-sacrifice for the kin constitutes, in my opinion, a different motive as it fits nicely with the kin selection theory.

Part III

Interactive minds

5 Reciprocal brain

Believe or not, we hiccup because of our "inner fish." Hiccups are caused by a misfiring of ancient nerve wiring—a reflex that helped keep water off our ancestor's lungs (Shubin, 2009). Since the evolution of our species has been painfully slow, some of our evolutionary adaptations (and maladaptations) are shared across many species and not unique to us. Reciprocity must be one of these shared traits—and one that emerged early in evolution, since we seem to share the tit-for-tat behavioral code with other animals, even with fish (Milinski, Kulling, & Kettler, 1990). Perhaps an even stronger argument for the innateness of reciprocity is that there are abundant examples of cross-species reciprocity, such as is observed between meerkats and drongos in Africa (see Flower, 2011, for more).

Concerning reciprocity in humans, we observe that many of our prosocial attitudes, like reciprocity and parent-infant bonding, became part of our ancestor's routine behavioral repertoire when our mammalian brain and the associated changes in neuroendocrine physiology emerged. As Wilson (2006) argues, "the parent-infant bond that blends self-preservation genetic kinship circuitry with affectional circuitry in a reciprocal social relationship is, in fact, the foundation for extended social reciprocity." There is a possibility that the neuropeptide modulation underlying mother-infant bonds and pair bonds may have been re-tooled for reciprocity (Berra, 2014).

Emotional bookkeeping, gift-giving, and market exchange

I find gift giving a fascinatingly sophisticated ritual. Apart from the economic activity it generates, it reveals so much about human sociality. I often find myself researching the prices of the gifts my older daughter has received on her birthday so that when it is time for her to return the favor, the gift she gives back would be comparable in value and would match the original in other attributes like considerateness. If this particular experience is not relatable, I am confident you have offered at some point to pick up the bill to return the favor to a friend who paid for your meal the last time around. This is the reciprocal brain at its finest: each favor/

gift (i.e., a reciprocal imbalance) generates a (literal) tension that remains unsolved until it is approximately returned (Cory, 1999). This is as true for impersonal exchange as it is relevant for friendship. You would be unsatisfied if you perceived your relationship with a close friend to be unbalanced in either direction. You might even feel resentful if your requests were not granted, or overwhelmed or taken advantage of if you feel that you are being asked to do too much.

The relative ease with which we seem to be able to keep a mental tally of the approximate balance of favors that we have with one another should be considered a strong sign that our brain has special adaptations for this type of social accounting. Metaphorically speaking, this module is probably organized like "T"-accounts, with liabilities and assets on either side, and supports complicated calculations, like the value of a favor (which is a function of the cost to the donor, the benefit to the recipient, and the degree of kinship). Maintaining such a balance is important, because the perception of equity in relationships has primarily evolved to provide protection against exploitation. If accounting is overly imprecise, there will be considerable opportunities for cheating. Social emotions such as guilt and resentment are thought to be effective in helping us detect (and act on) such asymmetries (Silk, 2003). Dickhaut et al. (2010) even argued that the modern accounting principles are simply an institutional embodiment of how our brain evolved to evaluate social exchange.

Given the brain's tendency to conserve cognitive resources and the demand that the record-keeping of favors would place on memory, the reciprocal balance in dyadic relationships most likely is maintained by a system of "emotional bookkeeping." The form on which reciprocity takes among the primates (e.g., in coalition formation) lends strong credibility to this position. Among chimpanzees, de Waal (1989) observed a turn-taking rule in the exchange of social favors, which seems to have developed to prevent lopsided accumulation of benefits. In particular, primates tend to groom preferentially those that groom them more often—an example of an "in-kind" reciprocation, which appears to be the most robust form of reciprocity observed among our evolutionary closest cousins. The temporal decoupling of benefits (e.g., grooming received) and costs (grooming given) among the primates is striking given that primates have a limited understanding of future events. Jaeggi et al. (2013) proposed that long-term contingency is proximately regulated by a so-called "relationship score" that is computed through a tally of past interactions, thereby reducing the weight of single events. How would natural selection choose a behavioral strategy (asynchronous exchange of favors) that is apparently so susceptible to exploitation? If they (i.e., non-human primates) are not cognitively sophisticated enough to plan their social interactions for future gains, what is the basis for primates' delayed reciprocity, which is fairly common, if one is patient enough to look for it?

Schino and Aureli (2009) provide a rather daring, but highly plausible, answer, one that has important implications for humans as well. Instead of episodic memory (which is limited), they emphasize that the simple formation of an emotional bond may be responsible for reciprocity for longer time frames:

> [R]eciprocity and partner choice could be maintained by a system of emotionally based bookkeeping that allows the long-term tracking of reciprocal exchanges with multiple partners without causing an excessive cognitive load (p. 59).

Emotions are the probable mechanism that facilitates bookkeeping of social interactions not only for non-human primates, but for us, too. Even more importantly, as Schino and Aureli (2009) argued, emotions are instrumental in helping convert qualitatively different favors (exchanging grooming for social support later) into a more comparable form. Consider a situation where Jane receives a traditionally gender-specific gift—an eyelash extender—from her brother Joe. You may recognize that reciprocating such a gift is rather more complicated than reciprocating a $20 gift card, because, obviously, reciprocating in kind is not a viable option. Jane must calculate the emotional value of the gift she received and return a gift that "feels" qualitatively similar. This is no simple cognitive exercise.

The exercise of choosing exchange partners is most likely guided by emotions as well. As a function of past encounters, I argue, we may have been primed to engage with certain individuals with a more sympathetic mindset. Eimontaite et al. (2013) simulated the impact of such priming (artificially induced in this case) on our tendency to cooperate with a fictional partner. When participants were manipulated to feel sympathetic, they were much more cooperative. So, it is plausible to expect that the exchange of services triggers partner-specific emotional variations and that our behavioral decisions are susceptible to the emotional states associated with each potential partner, which, perhaps, provide us with a (cognitively inexpensive) rule of thumb for the accounting of favors. The stronger the emotional bond, the more tolerable the gap between favors and counter-favors would be. Feeling obligated to engage in immediate reciprocity (either by returning or requesting a favor) signals—as is the case with market exchange—a greater social distance. It is not surprising that a request for immediate reciprocity would elicit stronger feelings of betrayal among mates and close friends than it would among partners whose alliance is merely goal-oriented (Shackelford & Buss, 1996).

Reciprocity in the market

Generalized reciprocity refers to exchange relationships in which there is no calculation of value or immediate repayment of the goods or services.

This form is common among close kin, and friends, to a lesser degree. So, reciprocal relationships take on a more generalized (i.e., altruistic) tone and have clear inclusive fitness benefits for the donor when they are directed to the kin. In these cases, some imbalance in exchange relationships is tolerated. Hames (1987), in a seminal piece, reported that among the Ye'kwana Indians, the mean relatedness of a household to the village was a reliable predictor of how much unreciprocated gardening help they receive from other households: the more related the household, the more help they receive, as their gene pool is more representative of the whole village. Another interesting finding of the study is that the households that are the least representative of the common gene pool tend to expect less reciprocity, as is evident by their decision to make larger-than-average gardens to hedge their crops against failure.

Reciprocal exchange also helps build larger alliances with distant kin, or even non-kin. For instance, the practice of giving *moka*, which is common across the New Guinea tribes, appears to be motivated by prestige-related considerations on the part of the big man who tirelessly work to facilitate it. (See the documentary "Ongka's Big Moka" for a truly vivid demonstration.) However, at a closer inspection, the practice of giving *moka* serves a larger role. It also aims to create a reciprocal imbalance and put the receiving tribe in as much debt as possible (measured in pigs for the Kawelka tribe) so that they would not engage in warfare against the donor tribe.

Based on these findings, it is safe to argue that a well-functioning marketplace, where goods instead of gifts are exchanged, originates in our inherent psychological tendency to reciprocate favors. In this sense, market exchange is a variation on gift-giving with one fundamental difference: it does not necessarily have the building of social bonds as its primary objective—which is the underlying motive for gift giving, as explained above.

Each commodity or a marketable service embodies a level of effort, labor, and creativity. The buyer must respond to this offering with a return gift of equal value, usually in the form of money that represents the value of the accumulated time, effort, work, and creativity of the buyer. In short, the market exchange follows what Cory (1999) refers to as the "reciprocal algorithms of behavior," but with one distinction: the subjective experience associated with receiving gifts has to a large extent been lost and, I would like to add, may be transferred to the pleasantness of the (social) interaction itself (e.g., cheerful bartender)—resulting in a form of transference. Playfulness, interestingly, is a trait we tend to value in a trade partner. PLAY, one of the primary emotional systems that Panksepp (1998) identified, motivates joyful engagement and has a critical role in a variety of pro-social operations of the human mind. In some cases, playfulness may elicit trust and attachment much more effectively than a more guarded attitude (Watt, 2017).

But these automatic emotional responses to reciprocal gestures are open to manipulation in market exchanges. A salesperson's empathetic behavior toward the customer when she takes the time and lists all the appealing qualities of, say, a water filtration system, tends to create, as intended, an inevitable tension in the customer: a sense of obligation to buy, ideally, proportional to the effort expended. Similarly, uninvited favors, such as the use of free samples in supermarkets, are likely to motivate feelings of indebtedness creating the obligation on the part of many people to repay the psychological debt (Fehr & Gächter, 2000).

Reciprocity underlies marketing strategies as well. Consider the interaction between physicians and the representatives of the pharmaceutical industry. Pharmaceutical companies' marketing efforts geared toward healthcare professionals accounted for most of their promotional spending, standing at a staggering $20.3 billion in 2016 alone (Schwartz & Woloshin, 2019). It would be naive, at best, to expect that the industry would invest huge sums of money in an activity if it did not anticipate receiving something worthwhile in return. Anecdotal evidence shows that the physicians felt insulted when asked if their decisions are susceptible to this type of marketing[1]. But researchers (e.g., Harvey et al., 2010) are convinced that even very mild favors clearly matter and have a subtle—and sometimes glaring—impact on our judgments.

Neural basis of value and establishing equivalencies

Reciprocal exchange and cooperation with distant (or non-) kin, which approximates the tit-for-tat strategy (Sahlins, 2017), is the behavioral form with which I am more concerned in this book. In order to be adaptive to extend social exchange to strangers, our brain must be equipped with some innate competencies, four of which I would like to touch upon here:

(1) a mechanism whereby we can establish equivalencies;
(2) a reliable error-detection mechanism for deviations from the expected outcomes;
(3) the ability to infer other people's mental states; and
(4) and self-control.

To assess what is more or less valuable to us, we should have a system whereby we measure value. It is not surprising that determinants of (exchange) value piqued the curiosity of almost every economist since Smith. This is probably because nearly every dyadic reciprocal relationship where the genetic relatedness is low must assume some common understanding of the relative values of whatever is being exchanged (e.g., favors, merchandise, etc.), either simultaneously or subsequently. Although not the first scholar to take a crack at it, Adam Smith (2003) once proposed:

> The proportion between the quantities of labour necessary for acquiring different objects seems to be the only circumstance which can afford any rule for exchanging them for one another. If among

> a nation of hunters, for example, it usually costs twice the labour to kill a beaver which it does to kill a deer, one beaver should naturally exchange for or be worth two deer. It is natural that what is usually the produce of two days' or two hours' labour, should be worth double of what is usually the produce of one day's or one hour's labour (p. 67).

The proposed principle for establishing (fair) exchange rates came to be known as the labor (or the objective) theory of value—elaborated and perfected by David Ricardo and Karl Marx later on. So, it is not surprising that, of all pro-social behaviors, reciprocal exchange may be the most intuitive for modern economists to recognize, since it forms the basis for our desire to engage in mutually beneficial trade, which economics exclusively studies today. Even unrelated selfish individuals, as the American evolutionary biologist Trivers (1971) demonstrated, would help each other out if there were a strong probability the aid would be paid back in the future.

However, our brain does not seem capable of computing how much value to assign to anything in isolation. There does not appear to be any convincing neuroscientific evidence for the existence of a common neural currency—or, as Ariely (2010) calls it, an internal value meter—that is used to independently value stimuli across a variety of contexts (Vlaev et al., 2011). Instead, given that even subjective sensory experiences (e.g., color) are biased by the surrounding details, it is much more reasonable to expect that value-based judgments are similarly context-dependent and rely on somewhat arbitrary local reference points (or a baseline), as predicted by the prospect theory (Kahneman & Tversky, 1979). For instance, the sensitivity to relative (rather than absolute) income—or inequity aversion, the sensitivity to whether rewards are distributed equally—makes the meaning of any monetary gains ambiguous: a two percent salary raise might feel particularly rewarding if everyone else got one-and-a-half-percent. However, we have no idea what a two-percent raise should feel like independent of the backdrop against which it occurs. Another reason why the idea of a common currency is problematic is the fact that different rewards are represented by different neurons because different neurons respond to different primary reinforcers (odor, touch, etc.; Sescousse, Redouté, & Dreher, 2010).

Our brain may not be able to determine independent value ratings, but it must, at least, be able to compare whether or not two items represent a similar value. Neuroeconomists believe that the orbitofrontal cortex (OFC) is where the neuronal encoding of the value of a stimulus or a choice takes place. Plassmann et al. (2007) provide evidence that medial OFC encodes how much people are willing to pay for various items during simple economic transactions. The intensity of the activity in this section of the brain seems to correlate reliably with the expected value of the choices available.

Padoa-Schioppa and Assad's (2006) well known experiment also appears to be fairly conclusive in this regard. They worked with a monkey and initially discovered the monkey's preferences for Juice A and Juice B. They discovered that the monkey was roughly indifferent between 1A and 4B, meaning it would prefer one unit of A over 3 (or fewer) units of B. Later, they measured the activity (spikes per second) in one representative neuron while the monkey was given different combinations of Juice A and Juice B. The OFC activity roughly coincided with the monkey's revealed preferences discovered at the first stage. For instance, the 1B+2A (equivalent of 9B) combination produced roughly similar effects to the 6B+1A (equivalent of 10B) combination, as expected.

Error, error, error!

Reciprocity is sometimes characterized by the following phrase: "You scratch my back, I'll scratch yours." Let us consider the phrase literally. It is implied that services of identical quantity and quality—assuming both parties have similar taste for back scratching and also are equally capable of rendering the service—are being exchanged. How does the brain react if the value of what is received is not in line with what was expected? Here I will extend the traditional views of context to include expected outcomes, as our expectations are a function of our past experiences[2], which are a form of contextual information. In the context of reciprocal exchange, how does our brain react if our exchange partner deviates from the norm[3]? Does the brain process betrayal in the same way it processes situations when we feel ripped off (e.g., we paid a lot more for that new car than we should have)?

Desire to trust

Trust games provide the most promising experimental design to study our reciprocal brain and find answers to such intriguing questions. In a trust game, the amount of initial money sent and the amount of the dividends to be paid back are both a function of the level of trust between the parties. If the game is repeated, it may be possible to trace what goes on in each player's brain when cooperation forms or falls apart. First of all, the evidence from trust game studies seems to support the reciprocal brain hypothesis: we expect that favors given will be paid back— until they are not. This is particularly true when we think we are dealing with cooperative partners. This finding is supported by the fact that activity in the ventral striatum, a reward-related region, is strikingly pronounced if the reciprocating partner already had a good reputation. But why do we find a reciprocal gesture *more rewarding* when it comes from a partner already expected to return the favor? Phan et al. (2010) offer an interpretation: "the value of social capital derived from interacting with trustworthy partners is 'built into' the vSTR reward signal at a very basic level" (p. 13102) In other words, interacting with a trustworthy partner is valuable and rewarding in itself.

Trust in the brain

But what about determining a partner's trustworthiness? Is there any activity in the brain that could reliably predict whether or not your trade partner will return your generosity? King-Casas and her colleagues (2005) wanted to find out. They zeroed in on a brain region where the intention to reciprocate the investor's generosity (i.e., taking the risk and sending the money) may have originated in the trustee's brains: caudate nucleus. It turns out that the increased activity in the head of the caudate nucleus reliably predicts the benevolent reciprocity on the part of the trustees. This region seems to receive and compute information about the fairness of a social partner's decision and motivates the intention to repay that decision with trust—before the decision is made. More interestingly, once the investor establishes a reputation for being trusting, something remarkable happens: "a temporal transfer of the 'intention to trust' signal from a time just after the revelation of the investor's decision (a reactive signal) to a time just before this same revelation (an anticipatory signal)" (p. 81). This shift may be taken to indicate that in the trustee's brain there emerges a reliable model of how the investor would react. In other words, the trustee is ready to reciprocate as she is nearly sure that her partner had already decided to invest with her. It appears that we want to trust by default before we have any reason not to. Given the role of the caudate nucleus (along with ventral striatum) in the learning process—controlled namely by comparing actual and predicted rewards (Haruno & Kawato, 2006)—it is not surprising that it has a role in learning a partner's trustworthiness.

Error processing: calculating without calculation

Now that we better understand how the brain processes and determines trustworthiness, it's time to get back to our original question of how our brain reacts to reciprocal imbalances. Neurotransmitter dopamine and several key brain regions appear to code reward prediction errors, which are triggered by a discrepancy in expectation (e.g., trust) and outcome (e.g., betrayal). These signals are used by the brain to constantly update our behavior and their role extends to the social domain as well (Joiner et al., 2017). The firing rate of midbrain dopamine cells varies depending on whether the discrepancy is a pleasant or an unpleasant surprise: if the outcome falls short of expectations, the firing rate decreases; if the outcome is better than expected, the firing rate increases. These signals are key for animals to learn about the reward value of the stimuli in their environment and, in turn, they become vital input for decision-making. These midbrain dopamine cells project to areas such as the ventral and dorsal striata. The caudate nucleus, part of the dorsal striatum, is one of the important recipients of these projections. It is of particular significance for reciprocal behavior, as it helps us learn contingencies between our own responses and rewarding/punishing outcomes. Thus, the region helps us track whether or not our partner reciprocates our actions in trust games (Rilling, King-Casas, & Sanfey, 2008).

There is one last important brain region involved in prediction errors in social situations: the anterior insula. When your goodwill gesture of trusting your partner is not reciprocated, or if somebody seems to be free-riding on your generosity, there is robust activation in the anterior insula, in a sense akin to a fire alarm going off. Considering the anterior insula's sensitivity to painful psychical stimuli and negative social interactions like exclusion or unfair treatment, we can understand its role in generating emotional awareness (Gu et al., 2014) that is, in turn, useful for self-preservation as it makes us wary of potential exploiters. Moreover, the connectivity between the anterior insula and the lateral OFC helps us change our behavioral strategy and engage in tit-for-tat by punishing the freeloader in the subsequent interactions.

Our brains are truly equipped to engage in mutual beneficial reciprocal exchange relations. That said, it is not naïve. Our reciprocal brain has a keen sense of deviation from expected norms and re-aligns its cooperative strategy accordingly.

Scaling it up

The practice of reciprocity among humans is not only pervasive, but is equally impressive, because we have managed to retool and scale up this reciprocal behavioral rule so that it applies beyond peer-to-peer interactions. Consider the slogan made popular by Marx (even though he did not necessarily coin it): "From each according to his ability, to each according to his needs." He envisioned the sentiment to be the main building block of a communist social contract. All modern nations have created some policies that are, in one way another, the embodiment of this ideal. Such practices range from disability benefits to various handicap rules. Those who are skeptical of welfare programs, I often observe, tend to frame the recipients, implicitly or explicitly, in the same terms we would use to describe freeloaders. Needless to say, freeloading is the exact opposite of reciprocity. The fact that assistance programs that consist of work requirements (e.g., the Earned Income Tax Credit) are increasingly popular is an indication for how embedded the ideal of reciprocity is in our minds and institutions. (See Corning, 2012, for a more extensive account of reciprocal institutions.)

Notes

1 Loewenstein pointed out that physician would engage in "ostrich effect" to justify their choices than admit that they have been influenced: "All of this research suggests that physicians who will personally benefit from recommending a particular drug, treatment, procedure, or clinical trial will have no problem figuring out ways to justify that decision as being in their patients' interest."

2 I would like to further argue that our brain must be forming and updating expectations, like how objects should move or how someone should react in particular social circumstances, etc., in an approximately Bayesian fashion at the subconscious level. I say "approximately" because the brain, in most cases, operates with limited time and attention, and, in turn, relies on many shortcuts to save time and energy. Our higher-order cognitive skills (e.g., probabilistic judgments), on the other hand, have a fairly dismal record in conforming to what we would expect from a truly Bayesian brain (e.g., base-rate neglect).

3 I use the term 'norm' because, if we leave out unintentional deviations, full reciprocation must be our benchmark in any social exchange situation among the non-kin of equal status. Otherwise, there will be no motivation to interact.

6 Mind reading

In one of episodes of the popular TV show Seinfeld, George Costanza, unlike his friends, appears to be deeply bothered by the fact that the security guard at a clothing store in Manhattan, NY has to stand all day and has not even been offered a chair on which to sit. He goes on to suggest to Jerry, who did not find the incident necessarily memorable or bothersome, "That's why I'm different. I can sense the slightest human suffering." George is not unique in that. To varying degrees, we all have that sensitivity. Humans, and other apes, to a certain extent, have the unique ability to put themselves in somebody else's shoes—an ability also known as intuitive/folk/natural psychology. This ability, often referred to as mentalizing or theory of mind (ToM), is supported by a network in the brain called, aptly termed, the theory of the mind network. ToM becomes part of the cognitive toolkit of all developmentally healthy children around the time they turn 4 (Kloo et al., 2010). If you happen to have children, you can easily spot the onset of this phase by the increased frequency of sophisticated lying, particularly about the incidents that you did not directly observe: "Of course, I washed my hands, daddy!" Your child has just discovered that she has a mind of her own, that the things she knows aren't necessarily known by you. Enjoy the ride!

Mapping the ToM region

Recent neuroscientific research has been able to pinpoint with great precision, a distributed neural system that most likely supports our ability to read other people's minds in social interactions and simulate in our own body what they must be feeling. For instance, Walter et al. (2004) found that the anterior paracingulate cortex is activated when we are trying to represent other people's intentions in actual or prospective social interactions. The very same area lights up if somebody looks directly in your eyes or calls your name (Kampe, Frith, & Frith, 2003). In other words, the ToM network has sub-regions that are dedicated to social cognition. This fact is particularly illuminating, since it supports one of the central themes in this book: social cognition is supported by brain regions that are engaged exclusively in social settings.

Our mentalizing skills have particular interest to economists. Consider one of the most popular tools in economics for studying strategic interactions: game theory. In some interactions, our best decisions (e.g., to continue with a certain strategy) are as good as our guesses of our rival's or partner's intentions. Many of our decisions are strategic in nature, so the ability to mentalize (or empathize, in certain cases) does not clash with our pursuit of self-interest; on the contrary, it is a pre-requisite. For instance, certain solution concepts, such as the Nash equilibrium, are meaningless—if not impossible—unless we can understand other people's motives and beliefs (Singer & Fehr, 2005). In some settings, such as the beauty contest game, advanced recursive thinking is indispensable (see Bosch-Domenech et al., 2002, for a comprehensive meta-analysis). In a basic beauty contest game, each player simultaneously chooses a number between 0 and 100. The winner is the person whose number is closest to 2/3 times the mean of *all* chosen numbers. If your head begins to hurt thinking about what to choose, you're not alone. Since we are put into a position of thinking about what others may be thinking, Coricelli and Nagel (2009) expected that we would need to tap into our mentalizing ability. They were right. First of all, they found that playing against human opponents, as opposed to a computer (whose strategy is random), activated areas commonly associated with thinking about other people's mental states: medial prefrontal cortex (mPFC), superior temporal sulcus, posterior cingulate cortex, and temporoparietal junction. Within this network, activation in the mPFC is what clearly differentiates the more sophisticated subjects: the higher the depth of recursive thinking (I think that they think that I think that…), the stronger the activation.

Social intelligence and mentalizing

How does this ToM network help us navigate games with one other player, such as the ultimatum game? Many people are quick to reject offers that are too low in this game (e.g., being offered $1 out of a possible $10). What would be their attitude toward mid-value (between 1 and 5) offers like $3? This is the question Polezzi and his colleagues (2008) aimed to answer. Not only did the recipients take a much longer time before making decision, the mid-value offers also caused enhanced activity in the superior temporal gyrus of the mentalizing network, an area known to be involved in perception of biological motion (Thompson et al., 2005) and processing socially meaningful actions (Todorov et al., 2005). Contrary to the offers that are too low or fair, mid-value offers must have motivated the participant to contemplate what the offer means socially: am I being insulted? Is he taking advantage of the situation? etc.

The unique social function and the domain specificity of mentalizing become apparent when we are asked to play a competitive game against a computer and to try to guess what it might be thinking. Devaine and colleagues (2014) made their participants believe that there were two versions of the game: one against another human being (hide and seek) and another against the computer (gambling task). In reality, all reactions were generated by so-called "artificial mentalizing agents" (an algorithm) with different levels of ToM sophistication. Thus, the task was basically the same in either case—guess the intention of your opponent to maximize your winnings—but the framing was different: a social frame (playing against another human) or a computer frame. The participants performed much better in the hide and seek case, outsmarting their rivals—except against the most sophisticated opponents. However, when they thought that they were merely choosing between two slot machines, the bank won in most cases, except when the rival's responses were randomly generated. So why did the subject's performance end up being so sensitive to the framing of the game? The most plausible explanation is the following: the activation of the mentalizing network in the social framing condition motivates us to seek intentionality and, in turn, helps us to find meaningful patterns in our rival's reactions and update our decisions in a Bayesian fashion. These results may be taken to imply that our attention is uniquely elevated by social mentalizing. We seem to be at our sharpest when we are dealing with others.

Are these brain regions involved in the ToM really domain-specific to mentalizing? This is rather difficult to prove. One possible route is to present subjects with a series of tasks completely devoid of any content that could possibly activate the mentalizing system with no social content. Instead, they could include tasks involving abstract concepts, non-social and affectively-neutral description of human features (e.g., height)—while scanning their brains. Then it would be a matter of seeing if there is any overlap between the regions associated with these tasks of non-social, objects-related reasoning, and the core mentalizing network (i.e., TPJ and mPFC). Van Overwalle (2011) reviewed the experimental literature for clues. He found that reasoning with mentalizing (e.g., inferring other people's traits) differs reliably from pure cognitive reasoning that does not involve mentalizing. Specifically, he reported that, while only 10% of the studies without mentalizing showed activation in the mPFC, 80% of the studies with mentalizing content did. Mentalizing appears to be a key component of our social intelligence.

Empathy and selfish-selfless spectrum

Our dependence on large-scale group living makes the meaning of self-interest rather ambiguous. Self-interest cannot be defined without the social norms that determine its boundaries. We deem many self-interested acts illegal. For instance, insider trading is prohibited globally. As though we followed the Kantian categorical imperative, we have decided that we would not prefer to live in a world where insider trading is an "appropriate" form of selfish pursuit. This may sound counterintuitive, but I would like to argue that extreme forms of altruism may look equally anti-social. Take the phenomenon of antisocial punishment (Herrmann et al., 2008), sanctioning Mister and Misses do-gooders who are guilty of taking pro-sociality a bit too far (by generously contributing in trust games, for instance). This lesser known form of punishment tends to emerge more commonly in populations where cooperators are less common and the rule of law is weak. Punishment of this sort possibly aims at maintaining the status quo—rather than at promoting cooperation (Rand & Nowak, 2011).

A more meaningful scale to characterize behavior is its degree of social appropriateness, not how selfish or selfless it is. I use the term "appropriate" in two, complementary ways: first of all, it refers to what is socially expected of us under the circumstances; secondly, an action is appropriate to the extent that is ecologically rational, as we defined earlier. The social appropriateness scale has a major advantage as it leaves room for cultural variation and treats social norms as a (context-dependent) baseline. In this sense, psychopathy does not mean a lack of outward sociality. A high-functioning psychopath would have problems resonating with others' emotions, but not with cognitive perspective-taking (Lockwood et al., 2013). This person could identify and even understand what another individual is thinking or feeling (Dolan & Fullam, 2004) but would lack the accompanying affective response. For instance, a real estate agent with high psychopathic traits could discover that not being truthful with her client would be against her own economic interest and choose not to lie, but all without necessarily being aided by the (inhibitory) negative reinforcement offered by social emotions like guilt. As is the case here, having the ability to represent beliefs and intentions of our conspecifics is a pre-requisite for displaying socially appropriate behavior (however, selfishly motivated it may be) and facilitating social exchange. Thus, although our social expertise in a world of emotional beings relies on our ability to understand the minds of others and predict their behavioral reactions without necessarily always sharing their emotions in real time, cognitive empathy without at least a minimum of emotional empathy could potentially lead to Machiavellian and combative behavior (Smith, 2006).

Needless to say, mutually beneficial social exchange requires empathy. Empathy helps us pre-empt the likelihood of negative emotions and comes on automatically when triggered by the relevant circumstances. Even imagining another person in a particular emotional state (e.g., fear) is enough to activate the associated autonomic (e.g., elevated heart rate) and somatic responses in the imaginer's body. In some sense, our ability to empathize appears to have evolved from a system that helps us represent our own feeling states. This system is designed to quickly vet affective outcomes of various events for ourselves, but most likely has been retooled to help us feel other people's pain. Singer et al. (2004) found common activation in brain regions, such as caudal and posterior rostral zones in the ACC—a subset of the pain matrix that is believed to be involved in processing painful stimuli—regardless of whether we ourselves or our loved ones were experiencing the pain. Our capacity to simulate other people's internal state, like how they would feel if they think that they are being cheated, explains why we tend to be much more generous in ultimatum games than what the rational-choice theory predicts. Not only do we not want to be treated unfairly, but we don't want to treat others unfairly, lest we experience some of their pain and rejection and anger.

In that sense, empathy is a useful social trait[1] from a self-preservation point of view (Singer & Fehr, 2005). It keeps, I argue, our behavior within the locally determined and socially acceptable bounds and, perhaps, helps us form a moral center on account of its potential inhibitory role. Conversely, unmodulated empathy could possibly lead to a decision paralysis or to behavioral reactions that are detrimental to one's self due to the asymmetry it can create in relationships. Thankfully, empathy is modulated. That is why we naturally expect our empathy to be selective and our empathetic responses to be modulated by context. For instance, I may not share your joy if it is a result of an illicitly gained reward.

What is empathy really for? Since through empathy we share the emotional state of others, we also share the motivational significance of these emotions, which allows us to predict the probable subsequent actions more precisely. Empathy is also a tool; therefore, it helps access relevant knowledge about our environment: you recognize someone's clear frustration as she attempts to open an apparently locked door, so you immediately move on to the next available door. Lastly, empathy likely helps facilitate more effective communication, social coherence, and affiliation via imitation (e.g., the chameleon effect) and, thereby, promotes emotional bonding (Vignemont & Singer, 2006).

Note

1 Although I do not have room to explore it in depth here, I find Paul Bloom's concern that we may be exaggerating the role of empathy as a basis of prosociality and public policy-making noteworthy. For instance, he argues that "certain features of empathy make it a poor guide to social policy. Empathy is biased; we are more prone to feel empathy for attractive people and for those who look like us or share our ethnic or national background. And empathy is narrow; it connects us to particular individuals, real or imagined, but is insensitive to numerical differences and statistical data" (2014).

Part IV

Key innate competencies

7 Emotional path to willpower

We are inflicted by present bias. Present bias is a temporal horizon conflict and is driven by the overwhelming salience of present rewards compared to future rewards (Brocas and Carrillo, 2008). However, as a species, we cannot afford to simply live in the moment, but instead must learn to operate in the shadows of the future—a distinctly human problem. Most of our decisions are inter-temporal in nature. Unfortunately, we're wired to find a donut more tempting than, say, a celery stick. Choosing the latter would have involved a sacrifice (e.g., passing up something more enjoyable) right now while it promises benefits that are not immediately realized.

The good news is that *Homo sapiens* are capable, albeit imperfectly, of exercising self-control by balancing the demands of their present self against those of their future self. Adam Smith's *The Theory of Moral Sentiments,* his first and relatively less-known book, devoted a considerable amount of space to the discussion of these kinds of internal conflicts. Smith was convinced that our default mode of operation to blindly follow our "passions." He also recognized that we were gifted with the ability to evaluate our actions from a position of an "impartial spectator"—the ability which serves as a source of "self-command" and brings our passions-driven self in line with the conventionally accepted standards of behavior.

How does brain process the demands of our present self and future self?

Our capacity for self-control is far from perfect and often, as we know all too well, goes awry. Sometimes, for instance, your night-self, Jerry Seinfeld joked in his new Netflix special *Jerry Before Seinfeld,* screws your morning-self by staying up late. What about getting up after five hours of sleep? The night-self is quick to reply: "Oh, that is the morning-self's problem!"

The tension between engaging in short-term gratification and working toward longer-term goals is present daily. It is truly a battle of wills between the demands of our *inherited biology* and our *enlightened self-interest.*

In one of the most illuminating, often-repeated experiments, participants were given some variations of the following question:

> Do you prefer $100 today or $102 next week?
> Do you prefer $100 in a year or $102 in a year and one week?

Clearly, these are identical problems: $2 is either worth the wait or not. As you can guess, however, present bias swayed participants' judgment toward taking the $100 today. However, the delay in the second case caused a "preference reversal" (Kirby and Herrnstein, 1995). Economists call such reversals in our inter-temporal preferences "time inconsistency." In fact, these two identical problems, except that they are framed differently, activate different neural systems in the brain. McClure et al. (2004) called them β and δ areas. The β area is activated for the choices where a monetary reward is available immediately and encompasses the following regions: the ventral striatum, medial orbitofrontal cortex, medial prefrontal cortex, posterior cingulate cortex, and left posterior hippocampus. These regions are associated with limbic and paralimbic cortical structures implicated in impulsive and addictive behavior. The δ area refers to regions such as the lateral prefrontal and parietal areas that are activated when making choices independent of whether the reward is available now or sometime down the road. So, this is the more sensible area implicated in higher level deliberative processes and cognitive control, which are swayed much less by the passions triggered by temporal proximity. This is also the area that makes it possible for us to see the value of deferred gratification at all.

Self-control takes cognitive effort and stakes claim on the already limited mental energy we have. There is evidence that the value of a future reward is calculated by lateral prefrontal and parietal areas of the brain, which suggests that evaluating the future engages the executive, more sophisticated, and more energy-demanding systems in our brain. This is perhaps why we are more likely to make, believe it or not, selfish choices or use offensive language when we are, say, engaging in a difficult numerical calculation. Self-control is particularly difficult to exercise when it comes to decisions whose benefits and costs are separated in time—the type of decisions whose numbers show no sign of declining as long-term planning seeps into every aspect of our lives. Thaler and Sunstein (2009) call the object of these decisions "sinful" and "investment" goods. Notoriously, Homer Simpson can never resist the temptation of eating a donut right now in the present moment. We cannot easily blame him for his self-indulgent ways as donuts are immensely and instantly pleasurable. Moreover, there is no immediate negative feedback like a headache that can clue Homer in to the potential long-term health consequences of repeated donut consumption. Decisions to go to the gym or save money today pose a different problem where the sacrifice (e.g., effort, foregone enjoyment) is immediate, but the benefits will not come until much later in life. And, again, there is no immediate feedback. We tend to get these decisions wrong: we over consume the sinful goods and underconsume the investment goods. Understandably so.

Top-down regulation of emotions

Our self-control problems are universal and could be explained by present bias which is in turn consistent with the demands of the immediate-return economic setting in which we spent most of our evolution. Those of us who can exercise a more reasonable balance between the needs of our present and future selves must owe our strong willpower not to our calculating abilities, but to our ability to envision what it feels like to be, say, old and penniless. This ability, in turn, produces the motivation they need to resist the temptation posed by immediate gratification. In a highly creative study, Hershfield and his colleagues (2011) found that exposure to visual representations of one's future self (e.g., your artificially aged portrait) leads to a more future-oriented behavior in the form of lower discounting of future rewards and higher contributions to saving. They attribute the effectiveness of their intervention to its ability to force consumers to temper the emotions they feel in the present to make them more in line with those they expect to feel in the future. This interpretation is plausible and also in line with Loewenstein's findings about the consequences of the "empathy gap." By a "hot-to-cold" empathy gap, Loewenstein meant the excessive influence of current (most likely transient) affective states on our preferences (e.g., crimes of passion). The "cold-to-hot" empathy gap, on the other hand, refers to our lack of appreciation for the future affective states and their relevance for our decisions today: "When one is not hungry, afraid, or in pain, for example, it is difficult to imagine what it would feel like to experience one of these states, or to fully appreciate the motivational power such states could have over one's own behavior" (2005, p. 49). So, self-control has a lot to do with the emotional salience of behavioral options.

Self-control and social emotions: emotions are more helpful than you think

One of the points I have been trying to make in this book consistently is that we should not be surprised that our brain becomes a lot sharper when we deal with other humans than when we solve problems that require logical abstractions. This is largely because we probably felt more competitive pressures from other humans than we did from nature during our evolution. The tension between immediate gratification and the pursuit of long-term goals is present not only in preferences for goods and services, but in our social relations as well. So, self-control when exercised successfully has significant positive social functions. It is not surprising that some sellers are extremely motivated to signal that they are here to stay (as opposed to making a quick buck) and, in turn, can get very defensive about their reputations that have built by containing their greed.

In their attempt to provide a more substantive account of constructive rationality by drawing on evolutionary psychology, Capra and Rubin (2011) highlighted the need to integrate social emotions in the model of decision-making. Social emotions such as guilt and compassion, they argued, must have evolved to help us override our initial impulses and short-term self-interest, particularly, in social contexts. Such emotions have most likely been selected, I argue, at the group level. This means that those emotions that motivate more forward-looking behavior are indeed adaptive only if there are expectations of future interactions. These emotions serve as immediate motivational proxies for expected long-term benefits of important relationships. Fiske (2002) calls this characterization the "proxy theory" of emotions because these social emotions operate as "present proxies" for the long-term cumulative future value of the relationships they help sustain.

The relationship between emotions and self-control is bi-directional and is certainly more complex than the theories of top-down regulation would have it. Yes, in some cases, self-control does mean the down-regulation of emotions. In other cases, we do rely on *emotions themselves* to provide the self-control essential for cooperation if deployed within appropriate relationship type (e.g., friendship vs. market exchange). The cognitive control route to self-control does seem to have a reliable neurobiological basis we can identify. The dorsolateral prefrontal cortex has been shown to be implicated in the cognitive control triggered particularly when there is a conflict among our goals (Carter & van Veen, 2007). It is involved, for instance, in overriding powerful emotional biases like when we delay immediate gratification (McClure et al., 2004). Exercising consequentialist (i.e., outcome-based) judgments in the context of moral dilemmas—which requires emotional detachment—does also activate this region (Greene et al., 2004). Cognitive control most likely works through reducing our sensitivity to those things in the current environment that have emotional value so that we can secure future rewards of higher value (Gifford, Jr., 2002).

Emotions also offer useful guidance for adaptive social behavior. Many emotions are the basis of intrinsic motives that are an advocate for our long-term interests and help us overcome competing motives advocating for more immediate gratification. Anxiety, a special kind of fear, is one of those emotions, which is usually triggered when we fail to meet a personal or moral expectation. Similarly, an uncontrolled display of anger derives its strength from potentially irrational and unpredictable behavioral reactions it might produce. You might be suspicious as to how useful anger can really be. Shouldn't we be better served if we just ignored the non-reciprocators and moved on to another partner? One potential answer would be the following: the capacity for anger is useful precisely because the relationships it is trying maintain *are* valuable. Anger signals that a defection or potential defection has been detected or sensed, and that the defection will not be tolerated. The message anger is meant to communicate would keep the specter of a spiteful retaliatory threat vivid in your partner's mind (Nesse, 1990). This characterization is also consistent with the role emotions, as I argued earlier, have as potent defensive tools against exploitation.

Emotions participate in the regulation of social behavior and motivate us to pass up temptation to engage in non-cooperative opportunistic behavior in Prisoner's Dilemma type interactions, particularly when our partner is being cooperative. Evolutionarily more recent emotions like guilt, shame, embarrassment, etc. primarily bring social behavior in line with the long-term interests of a social group, rather than the short-term interests of the individual person (Adolphs, 2003). However, the incredibly constructive role that emotions play in economic transactions is often overlooked. Robert Frank (2003) is one of the rare exceptions. He pointed out that moral emotions help solve commitment problems and, in turn, overcome self-control. For instance, a person who is sympathetic toward potential trading partners would be much less likely than others to resort to cheating—even though she would still find the gains from playing defect more attractive. The allure of the quick gain in the current transaction would be mitigated by the prospect of the immediate aversive psychological reaction that would be triggered by being an unfaithful partner. We would expect persons with the capacity for feeling sympathy for their trading partners would find it easier than others to stick with cooperation in repeated interactions where opportunities for cheating exist. However, we should not overestimate the stability of such traits and our capacity to trivialize the occasional cheating. We have a very adaptable amygdala—a brain region involved in processing emotions—which is sensitive to our baseline of dishonesty and, possibly, other self-serving behavior. Our amygdala's sensitivity to opportunistic behavior in making a present decision likely depends on the magnitude of such self-serving behavior in the past. In this respect, what Neil Garrett and his colleagues (2016) found is noteworthy: what begins as small acts of dishonesty can escalate into larger transgressions in the future because of the diminished amygdala response.

The fact that the emotional rejection of socially inappropriate behavior (e.g., pushing a big guy off a bridge to save five lives) also tends to be extremely quick (Greene et al., 2001), and probably does not require much effort. This quick and effortless path to moral judgments strengthens the case that emotions, as context-dependent as they might be, are a cognitively much less expensive path to the exercise of self-control.

8 Sapiens see, sapiens do (Monkey? Not so much)

Ostracism is perhaps one of our worst fears; our aversion to social exclusion helps to keep us in line. There is a good evolutionary reason for it. Darwin (1896) himself identified, in *The Descent of Man*, our motivation to remain in a good standing with other group members:

> there is another and ... powerful stimulus to the development of the social virtues, namely, the praise and the blame of our fellow men ... the heightened sensitivity to praise and blame and the accommodating emotions (e.g. pride and shame) no doubt was originally acquired, like all the other social instincts, through natural selection (p. 131).

We have much more insight into how social rewards are processed in the brain today. For instance, Izuma, Saito, & Sadato (2008) tested whether social rewards like a stranger's praise are anatomically processed in a similar fashion as earning money. A compliment or praise aimed at enhancing one's good reputation, they found, consistently activated reward-related brain areas, notably the striatum. Most interestingly, the areas activated when someone receive a praise overlapped with the areas activated when somebody receives monetary rewards. *Reputation is indeed a currency.* The fact that we care about our image in the eyes of others reinforces our pro-social tendencies and lessens the burden on external reinforcements (e.g., the legal system) to maintain our adherence to social norms.

Following the herd

The extent to which we would act in ways to protect our reputation and avoid social sanctions is directly and highly sensitive to whether there are other people in the room. So, you would not be surprised to discover that even the appearance that you are being watched could motivate you to act in more cooperative (less deviant) ways. Ernest-Jones, Nettle, and Bateson (2011) found that displaying posters featuring eye images subconsciously influenced people (who were unknowingly participating in a natural experiment) to remove litter from their tables in a school cafeteria more often than those who were not exposed. The emphasis we place on social approval and our reluctance to face social disapproval manifests itself in several commonly observed behavioral patterns, primarily, imitation and conformity. The main difference between the two is whether a group or an individual is being imitated.

Do we change our behavior when exposed to the judgment of others? There are two potential links between emotional and behavioral adjustments. People may re-align their preferences with the majority because of the affinity they feel for the group and satisfy their need to belong to a group. Alternatively, conformity may be driven by a desire to avoid negative emotions such as the fear of social exclusion or a sense of shame or guilt in having different opinions or tastes. There appears to be some neuroscientific evidence for the latter form. Many neuroimaging and electrophysiological studies appear to suggest that when individual opinions (e.g., ratings) differed from those of the group, the conflict with the normative group opinion triggers a sequence of neuronal responses that are capable of predicting the subsequent preference reversals (Shestakova et al., 2013). For instance, the activity in the rostral cingulate zone, the area involved in the processing of conflict, increases, while activity in the nucleus accumbens, an area associated with expectations of reward decreases. So, dissent feels uncomfortable, rather *very uncomfortable.* Moreover, social influences like your peers' favorite songs moderate activity in the striatum and vmPFC. These two brain areas are believed to work together to encode the subjective value. These findings seem to suggest that what others think tends to have a substantive effect on our preferences. Conformity works through the representation of value associated with particular stimuli like a musical piece at the neural level (see Stallen and Sanfey, 2015, for a more extensive survey). So much for the fixed preferences that the standard economic texts insist on advertising!

We tend to conform even when the group is wrong. Berns et al. (2010) showed that one's error rate significantly increased when completing a mental rotation task as she is exposed to the opinion of others. The mismatch between one's own ratings and those of the group seems to activate a region known as posterior medial frontal cortex (Campbell-Meiklejohn et al., 2010; Klucharev et al., 2009). According to Izuma (2013), the involvement of the pMFC should not be surprising considering the role the region is believed to play in detecting a conflict between an *ideal state* and *reality* and, in turn, inducing preference reversals.

Conformity has also proven to be a useful motivator as a social incentive whose effectiveness is unmatched by the prospect of saving money. Allcott (2011), in one of the largest field experiments ever conducted, tested the power of social norms in encouraging energy conservation. He arranged letters, The Home Energy Letters, to be sent to the households participating in the study. The letter provided the customers with their relative standing in electricity use *in comparison* to their neighbors. Based on their relative energy usage, they were assigned one of the following three grades from the most complimentary to the least: "great," "good," "below average." This non-price intervention helped; on average a two percent reduction in energy consumption was realized among the targeted households. If this gain looks small to you, it should not be. The prices should have been raised by whopping 11 to 20 percent to bring about a similar reduction in energy consumption!

I recognize a good idea when I see it

I remember a real-estate agent who secured his sunglasses to his chest through a buttonhole on his polo shirt. "What a brilliant idea!" I thought. My usual method of storing my sunglasses, hanging them down from my collar, had always been a headache. The ability to recognize a good example and mimic it bestows on Sapiens many great advantages such as the cultural transmission of useful information—which includes the knowledge of how to carry your sunglasses with a minimum hassle when you are not wearing them. This, again, is another form of social intelligence that could be traced back to several identifiable neural circuits in the brain.

We tend to imitate what the majority of peers do (which we just called conformity) or imitate the "successful" examples around us, which is the basis for prestige-based cultural transmission. In a stable environment, our inclination to imitate is a highly adaptive trait. As Boyd and Richerson eloquently put it, "... when lots of imitation is mixed with a little bit of individual learning, populations can adapt in ways that outreach the abilities of any individual genius" (2005, p. 13).

Among primates where social learning is commonplace and vital for survival, many skills are culturally transmitted. They tend to solve many practical problems of daily life easily without recourse to their creative intelligence—which is most clearly present if elicited in artificial situations (e.g., solving logical problems). The fact that we are intellectually lazy does not, apparently, pose a great challenge in our (or our ape cousins') routine lives. This is partly because we have been able to outsource a significant chunk of our cognitive load to our institutions, formal or informal. For instance, modern accounting methods allow us to preserve information about past exchanges outside our brain. This ability is useful because it alleviates a capacity constraint on memory and extends the life of common knowledge (Dickhaut et al., 2010).

We seem to have focused our intelligence more on manipulating social objects and less on physical tools. The vast primatological evidence points in the same direction. Anthropoid apes demonstrate significant creative thinking skills in lab experiments. However, there is no trace of any of their creative intelligence put to use in their natural environment, as Humphrey (2002) reported. Rather, maintaining a collective mind, where practical knowledge is stored and disseminated, is the key to the survival of higher ape species. In this sense, human society functions like a "polytechnic school for teaching of subsistence technology" (Humphrey, 2002). That said, such a social community would not come about without a keen sense of imitation—particularly between the younger and the senior members of the community.

Imitative drive is so innate and strong that it seems to be supported by a set of identifiable circuitries in the brain. A strong piece of evidence that comes from the experiments done with macaque monkeys supports the existence of a neural basis for imitation in the brain called "mirror neurons" (Rizzolatti and Craighero, 2004). These neurons are a type of brain cell that respond equally when you perform an action like lifting an object and when you witness someone else performing the same action. Mirroring is a form of internal simulation key to acquiring many motor skills. Hamilton (2008) suggested that children with autism are able to understand and emulate goal-directed actions, but may have specific impairments in automatic mimicry of actions *without* goals. The current evidence is mixed (see Hamilton, 2013, for an extensive review), but their inability to mimic may be explained by their reduced capacity for some mirroring functions.

If imitation is the basis of social learning that had survival advantages, such biases were probably selected because of the advantages they bestowed on those who possessed them. So, the pressure was on to make more and more refined discriminations about what and whom to imitate. However, it does not mean all biased imitation necessarily contributes to genetic fitness. Cultural forms that disseminate could include rain dances, fancy clothes, body decoration, burial rites, or any number of other habits that may not be serving inclusive fitness. Since we have the genetically in-built tendency to copy certain practices and individual, the maladaptive "memes" (that are cognitive and behavioral patterns) will spread just as well as the ones that actually help survival chances (Blackmore, 2001).

Power of mimicry

Human imitation is unique among the primates as it displays the patterns of both faithfulness and selectivity under different circumstances with the weight of faithful imitation increasing gradually over one's life span (Hodges, 2014). We tend to more carefully imitate social conventions. On the other hand, a task with a transparent instrumental goal leaves greater room for the individual's creative spin (Legare et al., 2015). In the latter case, we take the intention (or the goal of the action) as our guide assuming that it is obvious enough. For instance, if an adult turns on a light switch with her head instead of her hands, observing children are likely to imitate her action, but only if the adult's hands are free. If the adult's hands are occupied, then the children imitate the act of turning on the light, but this time they would use their hands (Gergely et al., 2002).

The former mode of imitation, the faithful kind, is the basis for what Veblen called "ceremonial values." Ceremonial values are vital because of their role in maintaining the social membership of many types of group, while the instrumental use of this imitation, if it ever had one, is significantly downplayed or has been completely forgotten. Veblen's *Theory of Leisure Class* (1912) is a depository of many illuminating examples of imitation of the faithful kind that have come to get detached from their ultimate (evolutionary) functions:

> "Manners, we are told, are in part an elaboration of gesture, and in part they are symbolical and conventionalized survivals representing former acts of dominance or of personal service or of personal contact. In large part they are an expression of the relation of status,—a symbolic pantomime of mastery on the one hand and of subservience on the other ... Manners presently came, in popular apprehension, to be possessed of a substantial utility in themselves; they acquired a sacramental character, in great measure independent of the facts which they originally prefigured" (p. 47).

Ceremonial institutions (e.g., manners) not only normalize some status relations, but also facilitate social cohesion and coordination. Veblen's notion of conspicuous consumption is particularly insightful as he recognized that individuals not only have an innate tendency to imitate, but they are also biased to adopt some cultural variants (e.g., wasteful consumption) rather than others. Humans pay particular attention to, preferentially interact with, and tend to imitate successful or prestigious individuals (Henrich & Gil-White, 2001).

Emulation, on the other hand, is the favored strategy of the chimpanzees when sufficient causal information is available. However, if such information is not available, chimpanzees are prone to employ a more comprehensive copy of an observed action. In contrast to the chimpanzees, children employed imitation to solve the task in both conditions, at the expense of efficiency (Horner and Whiten, 2005). The fact that chimpanzees are more emulative (i.e., goal directed) than the human children who proved to be more susceptible to blindly imitating the models used in the experiments (Carpenter, Call, & Tomasello, 2005) might explain why it was Sapiens that have managed to create more elaborate institutions. As a result, cooperative activity was scaled up via the use of artificial cultural markers of many varieties from religious affiliation to tastes. So, what seems to be a weakness—blind mimicry—has been, perhaps, the key to our species' success.

Part V

Pursuit of identities, tribes, and emotional connections

9 Human sociality in the market

Our elaborate market exchange system owes its existence not to our calculating brain or insatiable self-centeredness, but rather to our sophisticated and nuanced human sociality and to the inherent rationality built into our emotions. A society populated with individuals who are rich in anti-social qualities would not have conceivably achieved any cohesion. The institution of impersonal exchange (one-off or repeated transactions with those with whom we have no kinship ties) has come about not because we have been able to overcome our often-misguided morals that are designed for small communities or our short-sighted zero-sum economic mentality. It is true, particularly in singular transactions, that some of our instincts have become liabilities as our genes have proved to be extremely slow to adapt to our changing circumstances. But the modern economic system got helped a lot more than it got hindered by such instincts. It, instead, is built upon many of our innate social skills as a species that support our capacity for building formal and informal institutions. Thanks to this capacity, we have been exempted from many cognitively demanding tasks in managing our affairs.

In this chapter, I will raise and answer three interrelated questions:

(1) In which sense are impersonal market relations embedded in social relations?
(2) Can for-profit organizations exist without co-opting social norms?
(3) In which sense do consumption and work represent activities wherein humans exercise their sociality?

Social embeddedness of economic transactions

As noted in the opening chapter, we do not have two distinct personalities at our disposal between which we switch back and forth with ease. We do not check at the door what we should expect from a conducive human interaction, such as feeling respected, each time we engage in trade. This is as evident today as it was on the 3,800-year-old Babylonian tablet from the ancient Sumerian city-state of Ur in Mesopotamia, considered to be the oldest documented customer complaint known to man:

> When you came, you said to me as follows: "I will give Gimil-Sin (when he comes) fine quality copper ingots." You left then but you did not do what you promised me. You put ingots which were not good before my messenger (Sit-Sin) and said: "If you want to take them, take them; if you do not want to take them, go away!"
>
> What do you take me for, that you treat somebody like me with such contempt? I have sent as messengers gentlemen like ourselves to collect the bag with my money (deposited with you) but you have treated me with contempt by sending them back to me empty-handed several times, and that through enemy territory. Is there anyone among the merchants who trade with Telmun who has treated me in this way?

We can clearly see that Nanni, the author of the letter, felt insulted and took Ea-nasir's behavior very personally. The origin of the discontent appears to go beyond a mere loss of money. This is hardly surprising, since any social exchange has three likely primary *emotional consequences* because of their implications for pleasure, social acceptance, and self-esteem.

Pleasure

The first emotional consequence is associated with the outcomes and concerns the hedonic tones (or pleasurability) of these outcomes. This is the most common treatment of emotions in economics: "it tastes great!" Our choices are guided by the relative expected utilities promised by various items. Neuroeconomists call these expected pleasures *decision values*. They are signals computed at the time of choice that help us forecast the eventual hedonic impact of those different options (Fehr & Rangel, 2011). Decision values, processed in the ventromedial prefrontal cortex, take into consideration various attributes of the objects. However, as I argued before, valuation is not a purely cognitive exercise; it can't be. Only those attributes that lend themselves to meaningful affective representations could guide our choices. Other attributes that do not have any affective resonance or salience will be most likely be tuned out.

Social acceptance

The second emotional consequence of social exchange is associated with possible perceived social implications of the outcome—which is usually much more salient if the outcome is disadvantageous. As an extension of our social intelligence, we have a very finely-tuned *sociometer*, an internal gauge that is sensitive to any stimulus with social significance. And few things signal danger as loudly as does the perceived possibility of social exclusion. Outcomes such as getting passed up for promotion, being refused service, or not receiving a performance raise may be processed as (indirect) signs of social rejection (or, if inverted, acceptance), and, in turn, would have serious implications for our self-esteem—regardless of their material impact. Direct or indirect negative feedback on one's performance tend to reduce self-esteem and cause a greater activity in the brain regions that are implicated in processing social rejection, such as bilateral anterior insula and the dorsal anterior cingulate cortex, along with the mentalizing regions, possibly indicating a desire to figure out the reasons for the negative feedback (Eisenberger, 2003).

Considering the association between a drop in our conception of self-worth and the elevated levels of the stress hormone cortisol (McEwen, 2013), exchange outcomes that are perceived to be detrimental to our self-esteem (and, in turn, to our self-preservation) must generate feelings in the body as with our other physiological homeostatic imbalances. In this sense, self-esteem (as a gauge for self-appraisal) can be considered as an adaptive product of evolution because of its role in guiding our level of investment toward various social activities. It primarily prevents us from investing too much in social relationships that are lower in value than we can achieve in the social marketplace or from wasting our precious resources (e.g., time, energy) chasing unattainable social relationships despite the high value they could offer (Kirkpatrick & Ellis, 2007). Imagine you are interviewing for a consultant job at a first-tier investment bank. What would you make of a series of rejections? What would you do in response? You may re-direct your job search to lower-tiered institutions. In that way, the drop in your level of self-esteem (in the professional domain) based on responses to your previous job applications can help you discover your "niche of acceptance and rejection in the job market" (p. 423).

Social interactions

Lastly, the social interaction itself during an exchange, independent of the outcome it leads, is also subject to emotional evaluation. Otherwise, how can one possibly explain the phenomenon of consumer vengeance, where the consumer desires to "get even" with an exchange partner based upon a dissatisfying experience? This is the research question that Bechwati and Morrin (2003) tackled. Apparently, consumers engage in vengeful actions in different and quite creative forms. One may choose to get even by leaving the table dirty at a restaurant or by creating a brand-specific hate site on the web. The founder of the site walmartblows.com described his motivation as follows:

> Pissed off at Wal-Mart, I needed a constructive way of releasing my frustration, so I bought a silly domain name and designed a Web site

> dedicated to my anger. I have created this site in retaliation against Wal-Mart for their crappy customer service and for treating their employees like s–t' (quoted in Kucuk, 2008).

Dave Carrol went even further to air his grievances against United Airlines by composing a song, "United Breaks Guitars." The song went viral on YouTube in 2009, having been watched 19 million times since then.

Interestingly, what seems to trigger this vengeful behavior in most cases is not necessarily whether or not the customer's concern has been addressed, but rather how politely or rudely she has been treated (Bechwati & Morrin, 2003). (For a more extensive take on the emotional needs that we seek to meet in the market as consumers, see Ingwer, 2012.) Consumer vengeance teaches us that there are many social norms that underlie market exchange, such as interactional justice. When these norms are violated, a series of (sometimes welfare-reducing) behavioral reactions, not predictable within the confines of the rational choice theory, ensues. Seen in this light, one might suspect that fairness, perhaps, is more often an attribute for the manner in which people are treated in their interpersonal interactions rather than distributional or procedural outcomes of these encounters. (Mikula, Petri, & Tanzer, 1990)

Such resentment and retaliation following interactional injustices extend to the workplace. For instance, Skarlicki and Folger (1997) compiled a long list of acts in which the workers engaged in their pursuit of getting even with their organizations. The list consisted of taking supplies home, attending to personal business while at work, spreading rumors about coworkers, damaging equipment, and others. They also found that the desire for interactional justice is also a strong motivator of more compliant behavior:

> when supervisors show adequate sensitivity and concern toward employees, treating them with dignity and respect, those employees seem somewhat willing to tolerate the combination of an unfair pay distribution and unfair procedures that would otherwise maximally contribute to retaliatory tendencies (p. 438).

This is not a surprising finding when considering that personification and transference are two species-specific ways in which humans deal with the world—a tendency that reveals some inherent biases in our (social) cognition. In many cases when the organization is large, for the employee, the employer is a fairly abstract and diffuse notion that is most likely to be personified in the role of a supervisor (or even co-workers) such that it could have emotions and intentions attributed to it—a form of transference. The failure to conceive of market relationships independently of our socially-obsessed brain, such as our desire to be treated with dignity, would risk leaving unexplained a vast chunk of economic behavior (e.g., turnover rate). Consider online reviews. I enjoy reading reviews not only as a possible source of information, but also as an invaluable opportunity for sociological observation. If you happen to read the negative feedback given for otherwise top-rated contractors on Angie's List, a platform connecting homeowners with contractors, the first thing you likely notice would be a rather interesting pattern: many of the (potential) customers appear to be frustrated or angry because they simply did not get a call back or were not treated well by the individuals representing the organization—usually on the phone. Based on my observation, many such reviews must have been written simply to communicate a sentiment along the lines of "How dare you!" But don't have to take my word for it. I compiled around 1000 such reviews (around 170,000 words) from five different top-rated contractors whose overall ratings were overwhelmingly positive, and then I carried out a text analysis using DiscoverText, cloud-based software, to find out the frequent word pairs. The resultant word cloud clearly supports my hunch (see Figure 9.1).

Although I have not found any experimental evidence directly pertaining to how interactional unfairness is processed at the neural level, I would expect the brain to process unfair treatment differently than it treats unfair outcome, as neural activity during the evaluation of procedural and distributive injustice displays a very limited overlap; the anterior insula was the only area active in both situations. The areas that were distinctively activated when the rules determining the outcome deviated unfavorably from expectations, such as the ventrolateral prefrontal cortex and the superior temporal sulcus, are indeed more sensitive to procedural fairness considerations (i.e., whether the rules are fair) than to the inequality in outcomes (Dulebohn et al., 2009). This means that, if a manager wants to minimize negative emotional reactions to the dismal pay-raise decisions, she would be better served by (preemptively) communicating as clearly as possible the fairness of the rule/procedure employed in the process of making the decision. Such a policy would increase the likelihood of

Figure 9.1: Word cloud showing the top 25 word pairs based on negative reviews on Angie's List.

Figure 9.2: Word cloud showing the top 25 bigrams based on negative reviews of a large US-based employer on glassdoor.com.

organizational citizenship behaviors on the part of the employee—at least it would do this more effectively than would other organizational efforts like improving the perception of fairness in rewards (Williams, Pitre, & Zainuba, 2002).

The sense of fairness (or lack thereof) in procedures and interpersonal treatment tends to serve as a basis for our overall impressions about an organization (Beugre & Baron, 2001). The desire to be treated with dignity and respect is clearly evident in online employee reviews. The overall sentiment in these reviews signals that employment is more than a

Figure 9.3: Word cloud showing the top 25 trigrams based on negative reviews of a large US-based employer on glassdoor.com.

Figure 9.4: Sentiment analysis of negative reviews of a large US-based employer on glassdoor.com.

contractual relationship maintained by external rewards. I compiled all one- to three-star (out of five) reviews for one of the largest employers in the US on glassdoor.com (around 630,000 words) and again analyzed the text to discover the most frequent word groups, either bigrams (word pairs) or trigrams. Looking at the resultant word cloud, there appears to be two obvious conclusions: employees feel overworked and, more significant for the case I have been trying to make, not treated well, as indicate by the frequency of the word *care* (see Figure 9.2 and 9.3).

Secondly, I ran a sentiment analysis[1]. If one takes the results with a grain of salt, given the limitation of the methodology, words that tend to reflect negative sentiments—anger, disgust, and sadness—appear to be commonplace in a typical review (see Figure 9.4).

Co-opting social instincts for profit

Markets would not have been viable—or would have remained small, in some cases—if the organizations populating them could not have figured out how to use a set of deeply social instincts to their advantage or figured out how to avoid openly violating any of the strongly-held moral beliefs or social norms. Consider the following hypothetical memo that our local retailer Mini but Mighty sent to its employees:

> Dear employees: Recently, the unemployment rate in the area has increased due to the closures of several local businesses. As a result, Mini but Mighty's market power as an employer has increased considerably. To exploit this newly found market power and boost our profit, we have decided to reduce all hourly wages by $2/hour. Thanks for your cooperation. Sincerely, the Management.

If you found the memo careless, you are in good company. No employer, as Arthur Okun (1981) predicted, has ever made (or, I wager, will ever make) such an announcement[2]. A sizable majority of those who participated in the study conducted by Kahneman, Knetsch, and Thaler (1986) found it unfair for a firm to exploit an excess in the supply of labor in order to cut wages (or, similarly, to exploit an excess in demand to increase their prices). Moreover, the sizable majority found auctioning as a pricing strategy unfair whether in hiring or in selling. Even in the age of big data, many online sellers clearly refrain from using a completely personalized pricing strategy. Instead, they use the information to decide to whom to give discounts. When asked why, 100% Pure CEO gave a clear answer: "We don't want to cross the line where we upset our customers, but we still want to capture the customers that are not going to buy" (quoted in Tanner, 2014). The foregone profit from not utilizing certain business strategies, such as the first-degree price discrimination (charging everybody a completely personalized price), may be taken as an indication that some conventional norms have been internalized (or so advertised) by business firms in various forms. These norms function as social constraints on profit (Kahneman, Knetsch, & Thaler, 1986).

Organizational kinship and instinct of workmanship

Herbert Simon, a behavioral economist before behavioral economics was popular, provided in his various writings what is, perhaps, one of the most intriguing cases of how social norms are deliberately invoked by organizations in the market setting to complement the incomplete nature of employment contracts. After all, there is no easy way to monitor or control effort or bring organizational objectives into alignment with those of the individual. Employment remains a relational contact (i.e., open-ended and under-specified). Firms may try to exert authority over their employees' effort through financial incentives (*if-then* rewards), but this authority will never be complete. Financial incentives as motivators may even be counterproductive when applied aggressively, as they tend to reduce intrinsic motivation (e.g., people's desire to be part of something greater than themselves; Pink, 2011). Williamson (1975) made a similar point by proposing a distinction between perfunctory and consummate cooperation. The latter form of cooperation, he argued, involves accepting responsibilities and exercising initiative and tends to generate a greater alignment between the goals of the organization and those of its employees, but is unlikely to be sustained solely through standard employment contracts. This is why, as Akerlof and Kranton (2000) argued, social identity emerges as an important supplement to monetary compensation, since using money as the sole motivator proves to be both costly, because of its diminishing marginal impact, and ineffective, because it may crowd out intrinsic motivation.

In reality, many people do exhibit loyalties to organizations and organizational goals even though the effort expended to achieve these goals does not seem to be fully proportionate to the financial rewards received or to the organization's overall success (e.g., profitability). The ubiquity of organizational loyalty does not strike me as an anomaly; after all, in the achievement of organizational objectives, we often see organizational identification (rooted in the us vs. them distinction) and pride in work as key instincts to which businesses often appeal to motivate their work force (Simon, 1991). Motivation and performance are apparently too important to be left to financial incentives alone; tribal instincts must often be summoned to sustain organizations as viable units.

A few years back I came across a YouTube clip of what appears to be a store manager surrounded by a group of employees at a Walmart pep rally singing "We are Walmart" to the tune of Queen's legendary song "We Will Rock You"[3]. My thought upon watching this video was that these workers must be so poorly paid that the manager felt compelled to motivate them by cultivating some sense of community and kinship—one that they can proudly claim. Creating a sense of community and kinship may be an effective strategy to turn potential outsiders (whose allegiance could only be bought, albeit imperfectly) into "insiders who needs little monetary inducement to perform his job well" (Akerlof & Kranton, 2000).

In other cases, organizations speak to their employees' instinct of workmanship—their intrinsic desire to feel that they are being useful. Medtronic, a medical device developer based in Minneapolis, shares with its workers the stories of patients who have benefited from the company's products in order to help them feel pride in their work. Pride, when it is achievement-oriented, is a powerful pro-social emotion—and a fairly cost-effective motivator. The motivational potency of this emotion is most likely associated with the fitness-enhancing potential it served during our evolution. As a psychological adaptation, it represents an alternative (and less conflicting) avenue whereby individuals acquire, sustain, and signal social status and prestige (Cheng, Tracy, & Henrich, 2010)—an extremely strong motive, as argued before. In a rare study targeting the neural correlates of pride, Chen and his colleagues identified activation in two brain regions—the right posterior superior temporal sulcus and the left temporal pole—that are involved in the initial appraisal of socially relevant stimuli and in other aspects of social cognition.

To sum up, organizational success and the viability of large-scale economic activity would be enhanced if our sociality can be co-opted for organizational objectives. The ability of organizations to internalize social norms to foster a greater degree of citizenship behavior (going beyond the requirements of their role without an accompanying explicit recognition, materially or otherwise) on the part of their workforce is captured effectively by the term *social capital.* Since we often mistake our feelings toward our colleagues and those higher up in the organizational hierarchy for our feelings toward the overall organization, social capital has a significant *relational* dimension that reflects the affective quality of our relationships. As the saying goes, "People leave managers, not companies." The affective quality of our relationships takes on an even greater significance in organizations where the completion of tasks often requires collectively intentional cooperation (i.e., teamwork). In such settings, not all efforts are equally visible to the management or subject to recognition, even though they may be key to the team's success. An environment where individuals are motivated to over-perform tasks that carry a greater weight in their performance evaluation and under-perform those that are not represents a clear misalignment between individual and organizational goals. Therefore, organizational outcomes depend on the degree of loyalty, obedience, and functional participation (going beyond the call of duty) that the organization can elicit from its members. And this feat is more likely to be accomplished in an environment fostering liking, trust, and identification among individuals (Bolino, Turnley, & Bloodgood, 2002).

Trust, trustworthiness, distrust, and social capital

I will now turn to the role of trust, specifically, the trust between buyer and seller. As discussed earlier in the book, building trust tends not only to increase number of potential trades, but also to maximize the mutual gains from reciprocal relationships—or at least it has done so in certain laboratory experiments. Trust also has reliable neural correlates in the brain. Exposure to the online seller profiles that communicate high trust and low distrust, Dimoka (2010) found, tends to strongly activate the caudate nucleus, the putamen, and paracingulate cortex. Furthermore, sellers with profiles communicating high *distrust* activated the amygdala and insular cortex, regions that are implicated in intense emotions and fear of loss and that most likely motivate avoidant behavior toward potential harm.

Although our social baseline may be an initial inclination to trust, cues signaling distrust are emotionally much more salient (McKnight & Choudhury, 2006). Therefore, trustworthiness needs to be signaled very reliably and distrust should be diffused very quickly in order to promote exchange. Particularly, in the age of digital (and, thereby, ultra-impersonal) commerce, trust requires a more creative set of institutional infrastructures, one that reflects our social intelligence. Online marketplaces, particularly online auction sites like eBay, would have not have come about—at a time where the legal framework was fairly under-developed—if the sellers were unable to build institutions that engender trust, since such one-off transactions expose the buyers to a greater risk of opportunistic behavior. In such online environments, institutional trust becomes the most important tool for building trust. In a study done at a time where online auction marketplaces were still fairly new, Pavlou and Gefen (2004) found that the perceived effectiveness of feedback mechanisms (e.g., ratings) and escrow services, combined with buyers' trust in the intermediary itself (e.g., eBay), were positively correlated with the buyer's trust in the community of sellers in an online marketplace—even when controlling for the differences in trust propensity of the participating individuals. This form of institutional innovation is driven, and will be accelerated, by the fact that modern society includes many third-party private and public entities (or intermediaries), such as Amazon, Airbnb, and UpWork, who have a self-serving stake in promoting the number of trades among potential buyers and sellers. Such intermediaries would be motivated to preempt the buyer's unwillingness to be vulnerable to the seller who might otherwise elicit distrust, perhaps through incompetence or through possible social value violations (e.g., lacking goodwill). Promoting trust in the online marketplace still relies on more ancient institutions, albeit in a more elaborate form: online feedback/reviews have replaced gossip and reputation; the familiar faces of neighborhood brick-and-mortar shops have been replaced with online shops that have a permanent presence in our lives; third party entities that are not direct parties to the exchange, like credit card companies, offer paternalistic free-passes (e.g., zero liability) that are reminiscent of the safety-net once offered once by your parents. Perhaps, the more things change, the more they stay the same.

Expressive sociality and the market

The size, viability, and stability of market relations are dependent upon the extent to which humans exercise their sociality through (1) their choices of what/where to buy, (2) what job to work, and (3) their daily (playful) interactions with their peers in various organizational and exchange settings.

Consumption: "I buy, therefore I am"

The specific ancestral social challenges faced by humans, evolutionary psychologists argue, must have formed the basis for a set of fundamental motivational systems that function to help solve each challenge. These fundamental motives (e.g., avoiding disease) may be triggered by external or internal cues (e.g., somebody sneezing); they then coordinate attention, memory, and cognition in order to produce an adaptive response (e.g., refraining from physical contact). How would these archaic motivational systems translate to the choices we make in the market? Perhaps the affiliation system, as it is called—that is, the basis for our ability to build friendship and alliances for support—is one of the most relevant social motives urging us to seek brands and styles that help us fit in (Griskevicius & Kenrick, 2013). Thus, the complexity that modern consumption behavior has taken on appears to suggest that we are not in the market only to meet our psychical needs; we are also in the market to meet social needs (e.g., connectedness, feeling part of a group). Contrary to what might be expected, social considerations are not limited to a few conspicuous categories, but are as applicable to purchases of household cleaner as they are to purchases of a mobile app (Magids, Zorfas, & Leemon, 2015). In fact, the very concept of so-called "tribal marketing" (Richardson, 2013) emerged from the recognition of the fact that brands should fulfill the consumer's need to build connections and experience a sense of community—however, artificial it may be.

Beyond just fostering connection, consumption fosters identity. What you buy is also supposed to say something about you, a fact that American culture has noted—and made light of. Take again the beloved '90s TV show *Seinfeld*. The episode in question begins with George Costanza, one of the lead characters, scanning used vehicles in a parking lot at a dealership. He ends up getting tricked into buying an '89 LeBaron convertible (a clear violation of his preferences he had declared earlier) just because the salesman claimed that the vehicle was previously owned by Jon Voight, the accomplished and charismatic American actor—a claim which turned out to be wrong. Obviously, George does not fit with our typical utilitarian hedonist caricature, so the so-called "ceremonial motivation" (Veblen, 1912) behind his behavior is evident. He is not alone. Consumption choices are often instruments we use to fit in or to gain and signal status, in addition to the other functions they serve. To paraphrase it in mainstream economic terminology, "utility functions have been developed to express a wide array of non-pecuniary tastes and social preferences, such as the desire for children, the concern for status, and the desire for fairness and retribution" (Akerlof & Kranton, 2010, p. 10). These social preferences have biological roots in the sense that we preferentially adopt some cultural variants rather than others. We are very selective imitators.

Our obsession with what Frank (2011) calls "positional goods" is very deep-seated because of the significance of these goods in the Darwinian sexual selection process, even though positional consumption no longer serves the same inclusive fitness goals it once did. The fact that we are motivated to spend more on status-infused goods simply to boost our self-worth (as opposed to signaling fitness) is a clear indication that what we consume is intertwined with our self-image in the community, which is in turn connected to our psychological well-being. Sivanathan and Pettit (2010) identified four such therapeutic uses of status-good consumption: soothing psychological pain, as a source of affirmation, repairing bruised self-esteem, and as a shield for negative criticism. Apparently, when it comes to choosing what to buy what is at stake is much more than gain or loss of utilities.

Work: "I am employed, therefore I am"

> I'm more isolated than ever before. It is a combination of factors: I'm far away from where I grew up and went to school, I don't have coworkers, and going out is difficult when spending even an extra dollar brings about feelings of shame. Even phone calls with old friends and family are terse, and a bit tense. I invariably hear suggestions, or an offhand comment about "the lazy unemployed moochers" and I end up feeling like a liability even in conversations with old friends (an account of an unemployed person).

Not only in consumption, but also in employment, we see the powerful desire to be included and accepted. Unemployment often represents not only the loss of income, but of a social identity as well. Providing a social group membership is one of the core (but often less visible) functions of work and employment. Even increased perceptions of job insecurity are likely to lead people to identify less with the employed population, which negatively impacts their well-being negatively through a loss of social identity (Selenko, Mäkikangas, & Stride, 2017). Among those who are out of work, there are heightened signs of mental wear and tear. Based on the Gallup-Healthways Well-being Index, the duration of unemployment shows a positive correlation with the self-reported incidents of having or being treated for depression. In 2013, nineteen percent of those who were considered long-term unemployed reported that they were either having or getting treated for depression.

A job loss must be perceived emotionally similar to social exclusion, making the experience more painful than it would have been if it were only associated with the financial stress (e.g., temporary loss of income). The pain associated with social separation and rejection is no less real than psychical pain and is indeed processed by the same brain regions, as shown in Chapter 5 and 6. In fact, we are so attentive to the social cues that might be taken as signs of social exclusion/rejection that such a pain could easily be triggered artificially, such as in a simple ball tossing game. Imagine that you are part of a group three individuals who are playfully tossing a ball around. You start noticing an odd pattern: the other two toss the ball between themselves more often than they engage you. You might start thinking. "Something isn't right." Indeed, something is not. The toss pattern deviates from what you can explain by a simple chance occurrence; you are being excluded. If your brain were being scanned by an fMRI machine when this is happening, there would be evidence of activation in your dorsal anterior cingulate cortex—an area linked to the experience of pain distress (Eisenberger, 2003). This should not come as a surprise, considering the adaptive role of the anterior cingulate cortex in maintaining social bonds, even as early as infancy. As the authors of this study argue, "Because of the importance of social bonds for the survival of most mammalian species, the social attachment system may have adopted the neural computations of the ACC, involved in pain and conflict detection processes, to promote the goal of social connectedness" (p. 291).

So, work is more than an activity to earn a living; it *is* the living.

Notes

1 Although the appearance of emotion-related words, such as *disgust* and *emotions*, in overwhelmingly critical reviews is understandable, I would like to highlight the significance of one particular dyad, *surprise* and *anticipation*, as it may be associated with the feelings of resignation or fatalism—which is evident upon closer reading of the individual reviews.

2 This is a variation on Okun's example. His original example was about communicating a price increase by a supplier.

3 The clip can be found at the following link: https://www.youtube.com/watch?v=JOkQJm_UGM4

Epilogue

We may be cognitively lazy but our innate social skills are simply unparalleled. We are emotionally inclined to cooperate, if the circumstances are right, and our brain has a sophisticated error-detection mechanism that aligns our cooperative inclinations with the goals of self-preservation—which, in turn, prevents exploitation.

The fact that the role of trust that was originally designed to regulate personal dyadic relationships has been delegated to institutions has allowed our impersonal co-operation capacity to be scaled up significantly. Our capacity for building institutions is truly remarkable. Institutions from traffic signs to more informal rules like "first come first served" are indeed key to lessening the demand of our social complex life on our limited cognitive resources. Just imagine how mentally and physically overwhelming driving your car would have been in the absence of, say, traffic lights or divided roads. Many of us pay very little attention to what is happening around us while driving as we have delegated our "attention" to be performed, say, by built-in mandatory taillights in vehicles in front of us. Thanks to the modern infrastructure and our ability to institute a few simple but intuitive rules, we can rely on simple parsimonious heuristics designed for driving: stay in your lane; keep a safe driving distance; slow down when you see the red, etc. As a result, we are on autopilot for most of the way and most of the time. Think of the number of cars in traffic today as an analogy for the number of impersonal market transactions. Just as the number of cars in traffic would have remained very limited without the current regulating institutions, the scale of market transactions would have remained very small without us building a set of institutions reflective of our expertise in social exchange.

When I trace the viability of market system to our deep-seated sociality, I do not necessarily mean that we have a market-friendly nature. On the contrary, the avenues the modern economic interactions afforded us to exercise our sociality often create a false sense of social connectedness. We are driven to meet, rather unconsciously; our essential social needs (sense of belonging, parental instincts, etc.) through relationships that are somewhat superficial and transient. We engage in the transference of multiple forms. For instance, it is inevitable to feel some level of kinship with our co-workers and mistake playful interactions in our exchange relationship as a substitute for friendly feelings. Many of us feel connected but lack, perhaps, meaningful social bonds. Moreover, the market system appears to have invented new hierarchies, I should admit, in highly creative ways whose essence is captured by César Ritz's famous phrase: "the customer is never wrong." Although most businesses never rely on a single customer to service, they have interest in championing the fantasy that customer is always right. As a result, consumers are given an artificial social status that is usually reserved for people that are higher in the social hierarchy (e.g., elderly in some cultures).

Evolving market relations could push Sapiens out of their comfort zones in other ways as well. Consider the expansion of trade that has been pushing innovations in communication technologies. Despite having the best teleconferencing tools at their disposal, how should one explain the geographic clustering of IT industry in such areas as Silicon Valley? E-mail, social media, videoconferencing, etc. do not seem to have eliminated the need for face-to-face meeting. Why? "To defeat the human need for face-to-face contact," as Glaeser (2011) puts it, "our technological marvels would need to defeat millions of years of human evolution that made us into machines for learning from the people next to us … technology will never be able to simulate the full range of sensory inputs—eye contact, olfactory cues, the warmth of a handshake—that help live meetings work…" (p. 37). Geographical clustering is one of many forms in which our sociality pushes back against the demand for further impersonalization by the market.

I would like to note, finally, that a decentralized economic system that operates through decisions that individuals make might have some implications for political stability of the overall economic system. This is not a praise. Just an observation. Sapiens have a very strong sense of fairness to be applied exclusively in situations where grievances are caused by an identifiable party. An economy that is organized as constellation of markets may contribute to political and social stability as long as they are seen as *impersonal forces*. Our inclination and ability to assign the market a set of attributes that we usually reserve for natural (or supernatural) phenomena may be traced back to the cognitive revolution which, according to Klein (1995), dates back to 40,000–50,000 years ago. At this time, he argued, a set of profound changes took place in our brain that helped Sapiens live in a dual reality: that of concrete things (e.g., trees) and that of imagined (or abstract) things (e.g., nations) (Harari, 2015). For instance, without myths (e.g., corporations as individuals) that exist only in people's collective imagination, neither credit nor the Catholic Church would have come into existence. Therefore, in an economy built on decentralized decision-making, we are prone to believing that outcomes are generated by impersonal forces beyond any one individual's control akin to natural disasters. In comparison, the failure of deliberate economic policies could be traced back to those who have implemented them. In that sense, by diffusing the blame for many economic ills like unemployment, the market system may have become instrumental in maintaining political stability. This superficial stability may come at the expense of delaying policy innovation and limiting the political realm to address many pressing social problems, particularly in places where the myth of the impersonal forces is the most pervasive like the US.

References

Adolphs, Ralph. "Cognitive Neuroscience of Human Social Behaviour," *Nature Reviews. Neuroscience* 4, no. 3 (March 2003): 165–78. https://doi.org/10.1038/nrn1056.

Adolphs, Ralph, Hanna Damasio, and Daniel Tranel. "Neural Systems for Recognition of Emotional Prosody: A 3-D Lesion Study," *Emotion* 2, no. 1 (2002): 23–51. https://doi.org/10.1037//1528-3542.2.1.23.

Aimone, J. A., D. Houser, and B. Weber. "Neural Signatures of Betrayal Aversion: An FMRI Study of Trust," *Proceedings of the Royal Society B: Biological Sciences* 281, no. 1782 (March 19, 2014): 20132127–20132127. https://doi.org/10.1098/rspb.2013.2127.

Aimone, Jason A., and Daniel Houser. "Harnessing the Benefits of Betrayal Aversion," *Journal of Economic Behavior & Organization* 89 (May 2013): 1–8. https://doi.org/10.1016/j.jebo.2013.02.001.

Akerlof, George A., and Rachel E. Kranton. "Economics and Identity," *Quarterly Journal of Economics* 115, no. 3 (August 2000): 715–53. https://doi.org/10.1162/003355300554881.

———. *Identity Economics: How Our Identities Shape Our Work, Wages and Well-Being*. Princeton, NJ: Princeton Univ. Press, 2010.

Allcott, Hunt. "Social Norms and Energy Conservation," *Journal of Public Economics* 95, no. 9–10 (October 2011): 1082–95. https://doi.org/10.1016/j.jpubeco.2011.03.003.

Allison, Paul D. "The Cultural Evolution of Beneficent Norms," *Social Forces* 71, no. 2 (1992).

Ariely, Dan. *Predictably Irrational: The Hidden Forces That Shape Our Decisions*. Rev. and expanded ed., 1. Harper Perennial ed. New York, NY: Harper Perennial, 2010.

Ariely, Dan, U. Gneezy, E. Haruvy. "Social Norms and the Price of Zero. " *Journal of Consumer Psychology* 28(2) (2018):180–191. doi:10.1002/jcpy.1018.

Arrow, Kenneth J. "Rationality of Self and Others in an Economic System," *The Journal of Business* 59, no. 4 (1986): S385–99.

Axelrod, Robert, and William D. Hamilton. "The Evolution of Cooperation," *Science* 211, no. 4489 (1981): 1390–96.

Barkow, Jerome H., ed. *The Adapted Mind: Evolutionary Psychology and the Generation of Culture*. New York: Oxford University Press, 1995.

Baron-Cohen, Simon, Ruth Campbell, Annette Karmiloff-Smith, Julia Grant, and Jane Walker. "Are Children with Autism Blind to the Mentalistic Significance of the Eyes?" *British Journal of Developmental Psychology* 13, no. 4 (November 1995): 379–98. https://doi.org/10.1111/j.2044-835X.1995.tb00687.x.

Bechwati, Nada Nasr, and Maureen Morrin. "Outraged Consumers: Getting Even at the Expense of Getting a Good Deal," *Journal of Consumer Psychology* 13, no. 4 (January 2003): 440–53. https://doi.org/10.1207/S15327663JCP1304_11.

Beckes, Lane, and James A. Coan. "Social Baseline Theory: The Role of Social Proximity in Emotion and Economy of Action: Social Baseline Theory," *Social and Personality Psychology Compass* 5, no. 12 (December 2011): 976–88. https://doi.org/10.1111/j.1751-9004.2011.00400.x.

Bernard, Larry C., Michael Mills, Leland Swenson, and R. Patricia Walsh. "An Evolutionary Theory of Human Motivation," *Genetic, Social, and General Psychology Monographs* 131, no. 2 (May 2005): 129–84. https://doi.org/10.3200/MONO.131.2.129-184.

Berns, Gregory S., C. Monica Capra, Sara Moore, and Charles Noussair. "Neural Mechanisms of the Influence of Popularity on Adolescent Ratings of Music," *NeuroImage* 49, no. 3 (February 2010): 2687–96. https://doi.org/10.1016/j.neuroimage.2009.10.070.

Berra, Irene. "An Evolutionary Ockham's Razor to Reciprocity," *Frontiers in Psychology* 5 (November 5, 2014). https://doi.org/10.3389/fpsyg.2014.01258.

Beugre, Constant D., and Robert A. Baron. "Perceptions of Systemic Justice: The Effects of Distributive, Procedural, and Interactional Justice," *Journal of Applied Social Psychology* 31, no. 2 (February 2001): 324–39. https://doi.org/10.1111/j.1559-1816.2001.tb00199.x.

Binmore, K. G. *Game Theory and the Social Contract*. V. 2: MIT Press Series on Economic Learning and Social Evolution. Cambridge, Mass: MIT Press, 1994.

Blackmore, Susan. "Evolution and Memes: The Human Brain as a Selective Imitation Device," *Cybernetics and Systems* 32, no. 1–2 (January 2001): 225–55. https://doi.org/10.1080/019697201300001867.

Bloom, Paul. "Against Empathy," Text. *Boston Review*, August 20, 2014. http://bostonreview.net/forum/paul-bloom-against-empathy.

Bohl, Vivian, and Wouter van den Bos. "Toward an Integrative Account of Social Cognition: Marrying Theory of Mind and Interactionism to Study the Interplay of Type 1 and Type 2 Processes," *Frontiers in Human Neuroscience* 6 (2012). https://doi.org/10.3389/fnhum.2012.00274.

Bolino, Mark C., William H. Turnley, and James M. Bloodgood. "Citizenship Behavior and the Creation of Social Capital in Organizations." *The Academy of Management Review* 27, no. 4 (2002): 505–22. https://doi.org/10.2307/4134400.

Bosch-Domenech, Antoni, Jose G. Montalvo, Rosemarie Nagel, and Albert Satorra. "One, Two, (Three), Infinity: Newspaper and Beauty-Contest Experiments," *American Economic Review* 92, no. 5 (2002).

Bowles, Samuel, and Sandra Polanía-Reyes. "Economic Incentives and Social Preferences: Substitutes or Complements?" *Journal of Economic Literature* 50, no. 2 (June 2012): 368–425. https://doi.org/10.1257/jel.50.2.368.

Brocas, Isabelle, and Juan D. Carrillo. "The Brain as a Hierarchical Organization," *American Economic Review* 98, no. 4 (August 2008): 1312–46. https://doi.org/10.1257/aer.98.4.1312.

Camerer, Colin F., George Loewenstein, and Drazen Prelec. "Neuroeconomics: Why Economics Needs Brains," *Scandinavian Journal of Economics* 106, no. 3 (October 2004): 555–79. https://doi.org/10.1111/j.0347-0520.2004.00377.x.

Camerer, Colin, George Loewenstein, and Drazen Prelec. "Neuroeconomics: How Neuroscience Can Inform Economics," *Journal of Economic Literature* 43, no. 1 (2005): 9–64.

Campbell-Meiklejohn, Daniel K., Dominik R. Bach, Andreas Roepstorff, Raymond J. Dolan, and Chris D. Frith. "How the Opinion of Others Affects Our Valuation of Objects," *Current Biology* 20, no. 13 (July 13, 2010): 1165–70. https://doi.org/10.1016/j.cub.2010.04.055.

Capra, C. Monica, and Paul H. Rubin. "Rationality and Utility: Economics and Evolutionary Psychology," In *Evolutionary Psychology in the Business Sciences*, edited by Gad Saad, 319–38. Berlin, Heidelberg: Springer Berlin Heidelberg, 2011. https://doi.org/10.1007/978-3-540-92784-6_12.

Carpenter, Malinda, Josep Call, and Michael Tomasello. "Twelve- and 18-Month-Olds Copy Actions in Terms of Goals," *Developmental Science* 8, no. 1 (January 2005): F13–20. https://doi.org/10.1111/j.1467-7687.2004.00385.x.

Carter, Cameron S., and Vincent van Veen. "Anterior Cingulate Cortex and Conflict Detection: An Update of Theory and Data," *Cognitive, Affective, & Behavioral Neuroscience* 7, no. 4 (December 2007): 367–79. https://doi.org/10.3758/CABN.7.4.367.

Centorrino, Samuele, Elodie Djemai, Astrid Hopfensitz, Manfred Milinski, and Paul Seabright. "Honest Signaling in Trust Interactions: Smiles Rated as Genuine Induce Trust and Signal Higher Earning Opportunities," *Evolution and Human Behavior* 36, no. 1 (January 2015): 8–16. https://doi.org/10.1016/j.evolhumbehav.2014.08.001.

Charlton, Bruce G. "The Inequity of Inequality: Egalitarian Instincts and Evolutionary Psychology," *Journal of Health Psychology* 2, no. 3 (July 1997): 413–25. https://doi.org/10.1177/135910539700200309.

Cheng, Joey T., Jessica L. Tracy, and Joseph Henrich. "Pride, Personality, and the Evolutionary Foundations of Human Social Status," *Evolution and Human Behavior* 31, no. 5 (September 2010): 334–47. https://doi.org/10.1016/j.evolhumbehav.2010.02.004.

Cialdini, Robert B., Linda J. Demaine, Brad J. Sagarin, Daniel W. Barrett, Kelton Rhoads, and Patricia L. Winter. "Managing Social Norms for Persuasive Impact," *Social Influence* 1, no. 1 (March 2006): 3–15. https://doi.org/10.1080/15534510500181459.

Clayton, Nicola S., Timothy J. Bussey, and Anthony Dickinson. "Can Animals Recall the Past and Plan for the Future?" *Nature Reviews Neuroscience* 4, no. 8 (August 2003): 685–91. https://doi.org/10.1038/nrn1180.

Coan, James A., Hillary S. Schaefer, and Richard J. Davidson. "Lending a Hand: Social Regulation of the Neural Response to Threat," *Psychological Science* 17, no. 12 (December 2006): 1032–39. https://doi.org/10.1111/j.1467-9280.2006.01832.x.

Cohen, Jessica L., and William T. Dickens. "A Foundation for Behavioral Economics," *The American Economic Review* 92, no. 2 (2002): 335–38.

Cohen, Jonathan D. "The Vulcanization of the Human Brain: A Neural Perspective on Interactions Between Cognition and Emotion," *Journal of Economic Perspectives* 19, no. 4 (December 2005): 3–24. https://doi.org/10.1257/089533005775196750.

Cooke, Lucy J, Claire MA Haworth, and Jane Wardle. "Genetic and Environmental Influences on Children's Food Neophobia," *The American Journal of Clinical Nutrition* 86, no. 2 (August 1, 2007): 428–33. https://doi.org/10.1093/ajcn/86.2.428.

Coricelli, G., and R. Nagel. "Neural Correlates of Depth of Strategic Reasoning in Medial Prefrontal Cortex," *Proceedings of the National Academy of Sciences* 106, no. 23 (June 9, 2009): 9163–68. https://doi.org/10.1073/pnas.0807721106.

Coricelli, Giorgio, Hugo D. Critchley, Mateus Joffily, John P. O'Doherty, Angela Sirigu, and Raymond J. Dolan. "Regret and Its Avoidance: A Neuroimaging Study of Choice Behavior," *Nature Neuroscience* 8, no. 9 (September 2005): 1255–62. https://doi.org/10.1038/nn1514.

Coricelli, Giorgio, Mateus Joffily, Claude Montmarquette, and Marie Claire Villeval. "Cheating, Emotions, and Rationality: An Experiment on Tax Evasion," *Experimental Economics* 13, no. 2 (June 2010): 226–47. https://doi.org/10.1007/s10683-010-9237-5.

Corning, Peter A. *The Fair Society: The Science of Human Nature and the Pursuit of Social Justice*. Chicago; London: University of Chicago Press, 2012.

Cory, Gerald A. "A Behavioral Model of the Dual Motive Approach to Behavioral Economics and Social Exchange," *The Journal of Socio-Economics* 35, no. 4 (August 2006): 592–612. https://doi.org/10.1016/j.socec.2005.12.017.

———. "MacLean's Triune Brain Concept: In Praise and Appraisal," In *The Reciprocal Modular Brain in Economics and Politics*, by Gerald A. Cory, 13–27. Boston, MA: Springer US, 1999. https://doi.org/10.1007/978-1-4615-4747-1_3.

Cosmides, L., H. C. Barrett, and J. Tooby. "Adaptive Specializations, Social Exchange, and the Evolution of Human Intelligence," *Proceedings of the National Academy of Sciences* 107, no. Supplement_2 (May 11, 2010): 9007–14. https://doi.org/10.1073/pnas.0914623107.

Cosmides, Leda, and John Tooby. "Adaptations for Reasoning About Social Exchange," In *The Handbook of Evolutionary Psychology*, edited by David M Buss, 1–44. Hoboken, NJ, USA: John Wiley & Sons, Inc., 2015. https://doi.org/10.1002/9781119125563.evpsych225.

———. "Neurocognitive Adaptations Designed for Social Exchange," In *The Handbook of Evolutionary Psychology*, edited by David M. Buss, 584–627. Hoboken, NJ, USA: John Wiley & Sons, Inc., 2015. https://doi.org/10.1002/9780470939376.ch20.

Dalton, Kim M., Brendon M. Nacewicz, Tom Johnstone, Hillary S. Schaefer, Morton Ann Gernsbacher, H. H. Goldsmith, Andrew L. Alexander, and Richard J. Davidson. "Gaze Fixation and the Neural Circuitry of Face Processing in Autism," *Nature Neuroscience* 8, no. 4 (April 2005): 519–26. https://doi.org/10.1038/nn1421.

Damasio, Antonio, and Hanna Damasio. "Exploring the Concept of Homeostasis and Considering Its Implications for Economics," *Journal of Economic Behavior & Organization* 126 (June 2016): 125–29. https://doi.org/10.1016/j.jebo.2015.12.003.

Damasio, Antonio R. *The Strange Order of Things: Life, Feeling, and the Making of the Cultures*. New York: Pantheon Books, 2017.

Deacon, Terrence William. *The Symbolic Species: The Co-Evolution of Language and the Brain*. Norton paperback. New York, NY: Norton, 1998.

Dennett, D. C. *From Bacteria to Bach and Back: The Evolution of Minds.* Fist published as a Norton paperback. New York London: W. W. Norton & Company, 2018.

DeSteno, David, Monica Y. Bartlett, Jolie Baumann, Lisa A. Williams, and Leah Dickens. "Gratitude as Moral Sentiment: Emotion-Guided Cooperation in Economic Exchange," *Emotion* 10, no. 2 (2010): 289–93. https://doi.org/10.1037/a0017883.

Devaine, Marie, Guillaume Hollard, and Jean Daunizeau. "The Social Bayesian Brain: Does Mentalizing Make a Difference When We Learn?" Edited by Jeff Beck. *PLoS Computational Biology* 10, no. 12 (December 4, 2014): e1003992. https://doi.org/10.1371/journal.pcbi.1003992.

Diamond, Jared M. *The World until Yesterday: What Can We Learn from Traditional Societies?* New York: Viking, 2012. http://www.myilibrary.com?id=711854.

Dickhaut, John, Sudipta Basu, Kevin McCabe, and Greg Waymire. "Neuroaccounting: Consilience between the Biologically Evolved Brain and Culturally Evolved Accounting Principles," *Accounting Horizons* 24, no. 2 (June 2010): 221–55. https://doi.org/10.2308/acch.2010.24.2.221.

Dimoka, Angelika. "What Does the Brain Tell Us About Trust and Distrust? Evidence from a Functional Neuroimaging Study," *MIS Quarterly* 34, no. 2 (June 2010): 373–396.

Dolan, M., and R. Fullam. "Theory of Mind and Mentalizing Ability in Antisocial Personality Disorders with and without Psychopathy," *Psychological Medicine* 34, no. 6 (August 2004): 1093–1102. https://doi.org/10.1017/S0033291704002028.

Dubreuil, Benoît. "Strong Reciprocity and the Emergence of Large-Scale Societies," *Philosophy of the Social Sciences* 38, no. 2 (June 2008): 192–210. https://doi.org/10.1177/0048393108315509.

Dulebohn, James H., Donald E. Conlon, Issidoros Sarinopoulos, Robert B. Davison, and Gerry McNamara. "The Biological Bases of Unfairness: Neuroimaging Evidence for the Distinctiveness of Procedural and Distributive Justice," *Organizational Behavior and Human Decision Processes* 110, no. 2 (November 2009): 140–51. https://doi.org/10.1016/j.obhdp.2009.09.001.

Dunbar, R.I.M. "The Social Brain Hypothesis and Its Implications for Social Evolution," *Annals of Human Biology* 36, no. 5 (January 2009): 562–72. https://doi.org/10.1080/03014460902960289.

Dunn, Michael J., and Robert Searle. "Effect of Manipulated Prestige-Car Ownership on Both Sex Attractiveness Ratings," *British Journal of Psychology* 101, no. 1 (February 2010): 69–80. https://doi.org/10.1348/000712609X417319.

Eaton, S. Boyd, Beverly I. Strassman, Randolph M. Nesse, James V. Neel, Paul W. Ewald, George C. Williams, Alan B. Weder, et al. "Evolutionary Health Promotion," *Preventive Medicine* 34, no. 2 (February 2002): 109–18. https://doi.org/10.1006/pmed.2001.0876.

Eimontaite, Iveta, Antoinette Nicolle, Igor Schindler, and Vinod Goel. "The Effect of Partner-Directed Emotion in Social Exchange Decision-Making." *Frontiers in Psychology* 4 (2013): 1–11. https://doi.org/10.3389/fpsyg.2013.00469.

Eisenbarth, Hedwig, and Georg W. Alpers. "Happy Mouth and Sad Eyes: Scanning Emotional Facial Expressions," *Emotion* 11, no. 4 (August 2011): 860–65. https://doi.org/10.1037/a0022758.

Eisenberger, N. I. "Does Rejection Hurt? An FMRI Study of Social Exclusion," *Science* 302, no. 5643 (October 10, 2003): 290–92. https://doi.org/10.1126/science.1089134.

Elster, Jon. "Emotions and Economic Theory," *Journal of Economic Literature* 36, no. 1 (1998): 47–74.

Ernest-Jones, Max, Daniel Nettle, and Melissa Bateson. "Effects of Eye Images on Everyday Cooperative Behavior: A Field Experiment," *Evolution and Human Behavior* 32, no. 3 (May 2011): 172–78. https://doi.org/10.1016/j.evolhumbehav.2010.10.006.

Fehr, Ernst, and Simon Gächter. "Altruistic Punishment in Humans," *Nature* 415 (January 10, 2002): 137.

———. "Fairness and Retaliation: The Economics of Reciprocity," *Journal of Economic Perspectives* 14, no. 3 (August 2000): 159–82. https://doi.org/10.1257/jep.14.3.159.

Fehr, Ernst, and Antonio Rangel. "Neuroeconomic Foundations of Economic Choice—Recent Advances," *Journal of Economic Perspectives* 25, no. 4 (November 2011): 3–30. https://doi.org/10.1257/jep.25.4.3.

Ferguson, Christopher J. "Genetic Contributions to Antisocial Personality and Behavior: A Meta-Analytic Review From an Evolutionary Perspective," *The Journal of Social Psychology* 150, no. 2 (February 26, 2010): 160–80. https://doi.org/10.1080/00224540903366503.

Fiddick, Laurence. "Domains of Deontic Reasoning: Resolving the Discrepancy between the Cognitive and Moral Reasoning Literatures," *The Quarterly Journal of Experimental Psychology Section A* 57, no. 3 (April 2004): 447–74. https://doi.org/10.1080/02724980343000332.

Fiske, Alan Page. "Socio-Moral Emotions Motivate Action to Sustain Relationships," *Self and Identity* 1, no. 2 (April 2002): 169–75. https://doi.org/10.1080/152988602317319357.

Fiske, Alan Page, and Nick Haslam. "The Four Basic Social Bonds: Structures for Coordinating Interaction," In *Interpersonal Cognition*, 267–98. New York, NY, US: Guilford Press, 2005.

Flower, T. "Fork-Tailed Drongos Use Deceptive Mimicked Alarm Calls to Steal Food," *Proceedings of the Royal Society B: Biological Sciences* 278, no. 1711 (May 22, 2011): 1548–55. https://doi.org/10.1098/rspb.2010.1932.

Forbes.com. (2019). Different Customers, Different Prices, Thanks To Big Data. [online] Available at: https://www.forbes.com/sites/adamtanner/2014/03/26/different-customers-different-prices-thanks-to-big-data/#6a7676795730 [Accessed 16 Aug. 2019].

Frank, Robert H. "Commitment Problems in the Theory of Rational Choice," *Texas Law Review* 81 (2003): 1789.

———. *The Darwin Economy: Liberty, Competition, and the Common Good*. Princeton [N.J.]: Princeton University Press, 2011.

Garrett, Neil, Stephanie C. Lazzaro, Dan Ariely, and Tali Sharot. "The Brain Adapts to Dishonesty," *Nature Neuroscience* 19, no. 12 (December 2016): 1727–32. https://doi.org/10.1038/nn.4426.

Gergely, György, Harold Bekkering, and Ildikó Király. "Rational Imitation in Preverbal Infants," *Nature* 415, no. 6873 (February 14, 2002): 755. https://doi.org/10.1038/415755a.

Gerstenberg, Tobias, and Joshua B. Tenenbaum. In *Intuitive Theories*, edited by Michael R. Waldmann. Vol. 1. Oxford [UK]: Oxford University Press, 2017. https://doi.org/10.1093/oxfordhb/9780199399550.013.28.

Gifford, Adam. "Emotion and Self-Control," *Journal of Economic Behavior and Organization* 49 (2002): 113–130.

Gigerenzer, Gerd. *Adaptive Thinking*. Oxford [UK]: Oxford University Press, 2002. https://doi.org/10.1093/acprof:oso/9780195153729.001.0001.

Gigerenzer, Gerd, and Daniel G. Goldstein. "Reasoning the Fast and Frugal Way: Models of Bounded Rationality," *Psychological Review* 103, no. 4 (1996): 650–669.

Gigerenzer, Gerd, and Jurgen Rossbach. *Gut Feelings: The Intelligence of the Unconscious*. London: Penguin Books, 2008.

Gintis, Herbert. "Behavioral Ethics Meets Natural Justice," *Politics, Philosophy & Economics* 5, no. 1 (February 2006): 5–32. https://doi.org/10.1177/1470594X06060617.

Glaeser, Edward L. *Triumph of the City: How Our Greatest Invention Makes Us Richer, Smarter, Greener, Healthier, and Happier*. New York, NY: Penguin Books, 2012.

Gneezy, Uri, and Aldo Rustichini. "A Fine Is a Price," *The Journal of Legal Studies* 29, no. 1 (January 2000): 1–17. https://doi.org/10.1086/468061.

Goleman, Daniel. *Emotional Intelligence*. 10th anniversary trade pbk. ed. New York: Bantam Books, 2005.

Gordon, Robert M., and Ronald de Sousa. "The Rationality of Emotion," *The Philosophical Review* 100, no. 2 (April 1991): 284. https://doi.org/10.2307/2185305.

Gräfenhain, Maria, Tanya Behne, Malinda Carpenter, and Michael Tomasello. "Young Children's Understanding of Joint Commitments," *Developmental Psychology* 45, no. 5 (2009): 1430–43. https://doi.org/10.1037/a0016122.

Greene, J. D., R.B. Sommerville, L.E., Nystrom, J.M., Darley, and J.D. Cohen. "An FMRI Investigation of Emotional Engagement in Moral Judgment," *Science* 293, no. 5537 (September 14, 2001): 2105–8. https://doi.org/10.1126/science.1062872.

Greene, Joshua D., Leigh E. Nystrom, Andrew D. Engell, John M. Darley, and Jonathan D. Cohen. "The Neural Bases of Cognitive Conflict and Control in Moral Judgment," *Neuron* 44, no. 2 (October 2004): 389–400. https://doi.org/10.1016/j.neuron.2004.09.027.

Griffiths, Paul E. "Ethology, Sociobiology, and Evolutionary Psychology," In *A Companion to the Philosophy of Biology*, edited by Sarkar Sahotra and Anya Plutynski, 393–414. Oxford, UK: Blackwell Publishing Ltd, 2007. https://doi.org/10.1002/9780470696590.ch21.

Griskevicius, Vladas, and Douglas T. Kenrick. "Fundamental Motives: How Evolutionary Needs Influence Consumer Behavior," *Journal of Consumer Psychology* 23, no. 3 (July 2013): 372–86. https://doi.org/10.1016/j.jcps.2013.03.003.

Hames, Raymond. "Garden Labor Exchange among the Ye'kwana," *Ethology and Sociobiology* 8, no. 4 (January 1987): 259–84. https://doi.org/10.1016/0162-3095(87)90028-8.

Hamilton, Antonia F. de C. "Emulation and Mimicry for Social Interaction: A Theoretical Approach to Imitation in Autism," *Quarterly Journal of Experimental Psychology* 61, no. 1 (January 2008): 101–15. https://doi.org/10.1080/17470210701508798.

———. "Reflecting on the Mirror Neuron System in Autism: A Systematic Review of Current Theories," *Developmental Cognitive Neuroscience* 3 (January 2013): 91–105. https://doi.org/10.1016/j.dcn.2012.09.008.

Hamlin, J. Kiley, Neha Mahajan, Zoe Liberman, and Karen Wynn. "Not Like Me = Bad: Infants Prefer Those Who Harm Dissimilar Others," *Psychological Science* 24, no. 4 (April 2013): 589–94. https://doi.org/10.1177/0956797612457785.

Hanoch, Yaniv. "'Neither an Angel nor an Ant': Emotion as an Aid to Bounded Rationality," *Journal of Economic Psychology* 23, no. 1 (February 2002): 1–25. https://doi.org/10.1016/S0167-4870(01)00065-4.

Harari, Yuval N. *Sapiens: A Brief History of Humankind*. First U.S. edition. New York: Harper, 2015.

Haruno, Masahiko, and Mitsuo Kawato. "Different Neural Correlates of Reward Expectation and Reward Expectation Error in the Putamen and Caudate Nucleus During Stimulus-Action-Reward Association Learning," *Journal of Neurophysiology* 95, no. 2 (February 2006): 948–59. https://doi.org/10.1152/jn.00382.2005.

Harvey, A. H., U. Kirk, G. H. Denfield, and P. R. Montague. "Monetary Favors and Their Influence on Neural Responses and Revealed Preference," *Journal of Neuroscience* 30, no. 28 (July 14, 2010): 9597–9602. https://doi.org/10.1523/JNEUROSCI.1086-10.2010.

Heider, Fritz, and Marianne Simmel. "An Experimental Study of Apparent Behavior," *The American Journal of Psychology* 57, no. 2 (April 1944): 243. https://doi.org/10.2307/1416950.

Henrich, Joseph. *The Secret of Our Success: How Culture Is Driving Human Evolution, Domesticating Our Species and Making Us Smarter*. Princeton Oxford: Princeton University Press, 2015.

Henrich, Joseph, and Francisco J. Gil-White. "The Evolution of Prestige: Freely Conferred Deference as a Mechanism for Enhancing the Benefits of Cultural Transmission," *Evolution and Human Behavior* 22, no. 3 (May 2001): 165–96. https://doi.org/10.1016/S1090-5138(00)00071-4.

Herrmann, B., C. Thoni, and S. Gachter. "Antisocial Punishment Across Societies," *Science* 319, no. 5868 (March 7, 2008): 1362–67. https://doi.org/10.1126/science.1153808.

Hershfield, Hal E., Daniel G. Goldstein, William F. Sharpe, Jesse Fox, Leo Yeykelis, Laura L. Carstensen, and Jeremy N. Bailenson. "Increasing Saving Behavior Through Age-Progressed Renderings of the Future Self," *Journal of Marketing Research* 48, no. SPL (February 2011): S23–37. https://doi.org/10.1509/jmkr.48.SPL.S23.

Hespos, Susan J., and Kristy vanMarle. "Physics for Infants: Characterizing the Origins of Knowledge about Objects, Substances, and Number: Physics for Infants," *Wiley Interdisciplinary Reviews: Cognitive Science* 3, no. 1 (January 2012): 19–27. https://doi.org/10.1002/wcs.157.

Hirschman, Albert O. "Against Parsimony: Three Easy Ways of Complicating Some Categories of Economic Discourse," *Economics and Philosophy* 1, no. 01 (April 1985): 7. https://doi.org/10.1017/S0266267100001863.

Hodges, Bert H. "Rethinking Conformity and Imitation: Divergence, Convergence, and Social Understanding," *Frontiers in Psychology* 5 (July 8, 2014). https://doi.org/10.3389/fpsyg.2014.00726.

Horner, Victoria, and Andrew Whiten. "Causal Knowledge and Imitation/Emulation Switching in Chimpanzees (Pan Troglodytes) and Children (Homo Sapiens)," *Animal Cognition* 8, no. 3 (July 2005): 164–81. https://doi.org/10.1007/s10071-004-0239-6.

Hsee, Christopher K. "The Evaluability Hypothesis: An Explanation for Preference Reversals between Joint and Separate Evaluations of Alternatives," *Organizational Behavior and Human Decision Processes* 67, no. 3 (September 1996): 247–57. https://doi.org/10.1006/obhd.1996.0077.

Humphrey, Nicholas. *The Inner Eye*. Oxford; New York: Oxford University Press, 2002.

Inc, Gallup. "In U.S., Depression Rates Higher for Long-Term Unemployed," Gallup.com. Accessed March 26, 2019. https://news.gallup.com/poll/171044/depression-rates-higher-among-long-term-unemployed.aspx.

Ingwer, M. The Hidden Emotional Needs behind Our Decisions. In *Empathetic Marketing*. Palgrave Macmillan, New York, 2012. https://doi.org/10.1007/978-1-137-51200-0_2

Izuma, Keise. "The Neural Basis of Social Influence and Attitude Change," *Current Opinion in Neurobiology* 23, no. 3 (June 2013): 456–62. https://doi.org/10.1016/j.conb.2013.03.009.

Izuma, Keise, Daisuke N. Saito, and Norihiro Sadato. "Processing of Social and Monetary Rewards in the Human Striatum," *Neuron* 58, no. 2 (April 2008): 284–94. https://doi.org/10.1016/j.neuron.2008.03.020.

Jaeggi, Adrian V., Evelien De Groot, Jeroen M.G. Stevens, and Carel P. Van Schaik. "Mechanisms of Reciprocity in Primates: Testing for Short-Term Contingency of Grooming and Food Sharing in Bonobos and Chimpanzees," *Evolution and Human Behavior* 34, no. 2 (March 2013): 69–77. https://doi.org/10.1016/j.evolhumbehav.2012.09.005.

Johnson, Allen W., and Timothy Earle. *The Evolution of Human Societies: From Foraging Group to Agrarian State*. 2. ed., [Nachdr.]. Stanford, California: Stanford University Press, 2006.

Joiner, Jessica, Matthew Piva, Courtney Turrin, and Steve W. C. Chang. "Social Learning through Prediction Error in the Brain," *Npj Science of Learning* 2, no. 1 (June 16, 2017): 8. https://doi.org/10.1038/s41539-017-0009-2.

Kahneman, Daniel. *Thinking, Fast and Slow*. 1st pbk. ed. New York: Farrar, Straus and Giroux, 2013.

Kahneman, Daniel, Jack L. Knetsch, and Richard Thaler. "Fairness as a Constraint on Profit Seeking: Entitlements in the Market," *The American Economic Review* 76, no. 4 (1986): 728–41.

Kahneman, Daniel, and Amos Tversky. "Prospect Theory: An Analysis of Decision under Risk," *Econometrica* 47, no. 2 (March 1979): 263. https://doi.org/10.2307/1914185.

Kampe, Knut K. W., Chris D. Frith, and Uta Frith. "'Hey John': Signals Conveying Communicative Intention toward the Self Activate Brain Regions Associated with 'Mentalizing,' Regardless of Modality," *The Journal of Neuroscience* 23, no. 12 (June 15, 2003): 5258–63. https://doi.org/10.1523/JNEUROSCI. 23-12-05258.2003.

King-Casas, B., et al. "Getting to Know You: Reputation and Trust in a Two-Person Economic Exchange," *Science* 308, no. 5718 (April 1, 2005): 78–83. https://doi.org/10.1126/science.1108062.

Kirby, Kris N., and R. J. Herrnstein. "Preference Reversals Due to Myopic Discounting of Delayed Reward," *Psychological Science* 6, no. 2 (March 1995): 83–89. https://doi.org/10.1111/j.1467-9280.1995.tb00311.x.

Kirkpatrick, Lee A., and Bruce J. Ellis. "An Evolutionary-Psychological Approach to Self-Esteem: Multiple Domains and Multiple Functions," In *Blackwell Handbook of Social Psychology: Interpersonal Processes*, edited by Garth J. O. Fletcher and Margaret S. Clark, 409–36. Malden, MA, USA: Blackwell Publishers Ltd, 2007. https://doi.org/10.1002/9780470998557.ch16.

Klein, Richard G. "Anatomy, Behavior, and Modern Human Origins," *Journal of World Prehistory* 9, no. 2 (June 1, 1995): 167–98. https://doi.org/10.1007/BF02221838.

Kloo, Daniela, Josef Perner, Markus Aichhorn, and Nicola Schmidhuber. "Perspective Taking and Cognitive Flexibility in the Dimensional Change Card Sorting

(DCCS) Task," *Cognitive Development* 25, no. 3 (July 2010): 208–17. https://doi.org/10.1016/j.cogdev.2010.06.001.

Klucharev, Vasily, Kaisa Hytönen, Mark Rijpkema, Ale Smidts, and Guillén Fernández. "Reinforcement Learning Signal Predicts Social Conformity," *Neuron* 61, no. 1 (January 15, 2009): 140–51. https://doi.org/10.1016/j.neuron.2008.11.027.

Knaapila, Antti, Hely Tuorila, Karri Silventoinen, Kaisu Keskitalo, Mikko Kallela, Maija Wessman, Leena Peltonen, Lynn F. Cherkas, Tim D. Spector, and Markus Perola. "Food Neophobia Shows Heritable Variation in Humans," *Physiology & Behavior* 91, no. 5 (August 2007): 573–78. https://doi.org/10.1016/j.physbeh.2007.03.019.

Koppl, Roger. "Economics Evolving: An Introduction to the Volume," In *Evolutionary Psychology and Economic Theory*, 1–16, n.d.

Kucuk, S. Umit. "Negative Double Jeopardy: The Role of Anti-Brand Sites on the Internet," *Journal of Brand Management* 15, no. 3 (January 2008): 209–22. https://doi.org/10.1057/palgrave.bm.2550100.

Kurzban, R., and D. Houser. "Experiments Investigating Cooperative Types in Humans: A Complement to Evolutionary Theory and Simulations," *Proceedings of the National Academy of Sciences* 102, no. 5 (February 1, 2005): 1803–7. https://doi.org/10.1073/pnas.0408759102.

Lachat, Fanny, Laurent Hugueville, Jean-Didier Lemaréchal, Laurence Conty, and Nathalie George. "Oscillatory Brain Correlates of Live Joint Attention: A Dual-EEG Study," *Frontiers in Human Neuroscience* 6 (2012). https://doi.org/10.3389/fnhum.2012.00156.

Lawler, Edward J., Shane R. Thye, and Jeongkoo Yoon. "Social Exchange and Micro Social Order," *American Sociological Review* 73, no. 4 (August 2008): 519–42. https://doi.org/10.1177/000312240807300401.

LeDoux, Joseph E. *The Emotional Brain: The Mysterious Underpinnings of Emotional Life*. The Emotional Brain: The Mysterious Underpinnings of Emotional Life. New York, NY, US: Simon & Schuster, 1996.

Legare, Cristine H., Nicole J. Wen, Patricia A. Herrmann, and Harvey Whitehouse. "Imitative Flexibility and the Development of Cultural Learning," *Cognition* 142 (September 2015): 351–61. https://doi.org/10.1016/j.cognition.2015.05.020.

Lerner, Jennifer S., and Dacher Keltner. "Beyond valence: Toward a model of emotion-specific influences on judgement and choice." *Cognition & Emotion* 14.4 (2000): 473–93. https://doi.org/10.1080/026999300402763

Liotti, M., and Panksepp, J. "Imaging Human Emotions and Affective Feelings: Implications for Biological Psychiatry," In J. Panksepp (Ed.), *Textbook of Biological Psychiatry*, New York, NY : Wiley, (2004): 33-74.

Lo, Andrew W. *Adaptive Markets: Financial Evolution at the Speed of Thought*. Princeton, NJ: Princeton University Press, 2017.

Lockwood, Patricia L., Geoffrey Bird, Madeleine Bridge, and Essi Viding. "Dissecting Empathy: High Levels of Psychopathic and Autistic Traits Are Characterized by Difficulties in Different Social Information Processing Domains," *Frontiers in Human Neuroscience* 7 (2013). https://doi.org/10.3389/fnhum.2013.00760.

Loewenstein, George. "Emotions in Economic Theory and Economic Behavior," *American Economic Review* 90, no. 2 (May 2000): 426–32. https://doi.org/10.1257/aer.90.2.426.

———. "Hot-Cold Empathy Gaps and Medical Decision Making," *Health Psychology* 24, no. 4, Suppl (2005): S49–56. https://doi.org/10.1037/0278-6133.24.4.S49.

Magids, Scott, Alan Zorfas, and Daniel Leemon. "A Better Way to Drive Growth and Profitability," *Harvard Business Review* (Nov, 2015). [online] Available at: https://hbr.org/2015/11/the-new-science-of-customer-emotions [Accessed April 1, 2019].

Mankiw, N. Gregory. *Principles of Economics*. Seventh edition. Stamford, CT: Cengage Learning, 2015.

Mars, Rogier B., Franz-Xaver Neubert, MaryAnn P. Noonan, Jerome Sallet, Ivan Toni, and Matthew F. S. Rushworth. "On the Relationship between the 'Default Mode Network' and the 'Social Brain.'" *Frontiers in Human Neuroscience* 6 (2012). https://doi.org/10.3389/fnhum.2012.00189.

McCloskey, Michael. "Intuitive Physics. (Illustration)," *Scientific American* 248 (1983).

McClure, S. M., D. I. Laibson, G. Loewenstein, and J. D. Cohen. "Separate Neural Systems Value Immediate and Delayed Monetary Rewards," *Science* 306, no. 5695 (October 15, 2004): 503–7. https://doi.org/10.1126/science.1100907.

McEwen, Bruce S. "The Brain on Stress: Toward an Integrative Approach to Brain, Body and Behavior," *Perspectives on Psychological Science : A Journal of the Association for Psychological Science* 8, no. 6 (November 1, 2013): 673–75. https://doi.org/10.1177/1745691613506907.

McFadden, Daniel. "Free Markets and Fettered Consumers," *American Economic Review* 96, no. 1 (February 2006): 5–29. https://doi.org/10.1257/000282806776157542.

McKnight, D. Harrison, and Vivek Choudhury. "Distrust and trust in B2C e-commerce: Do they differ?" In *Proceedings of the 8th international conference on Electronic commerce: The new e-commerce: innovations for conquering current barriers, obstacles and limitations to conducting successful business on the internet*, pp. 482–491. ACM, 2006.

Mikula, Gerold, Birgit Petri, and Norbert Tanzer. "What People Regard as Unjust: Types and Structures of Everyday Experiences of Injustice," *European Journal of Social Psychology* 20, no. 2 (March 1990): 133–49. https://doi.org/10.1002/ejsp.2420200205.

Milinski, Manfred, David Kulling, and Rolf Kettler. "Tit for Tat: Sticklebacks (Gasterosteus Aculeatus) 'Trusting' a Cooperating Partner," *Behavioral Ecology* 1, no. 1 (1990): 7–11. https://doi.org/10.1093/beheco/1.1.7.

Morris, Michael W., Oliver J. Sheldon, Daniel R. Ames, and Maia J. Young. "Metaphors and the Market: Consequences and Preconditions of Agent and Object Metaphors in Stock Market Commentary," *Organizational Behavior and Human Decision Processes* 102, no. 2 (March 2007): 174–92. https://doi.org/10.1016/j.obhdp.2006.03.001.

Nesse, Randolph M. "Evolutionary Explanations of Emotions," *Human Nature* 1, no. 3 (September 1990): 261–89. https://doi.org/10.1007/BF02733986.

Nguyen, Tanya T., Tomasz Kosciolek, Yadira Maldonado, Rebecca E. Daly, Averria Sirkin Martin, Daniel McDonald, Rob Knight, and Dilip V. Jeste. "Differences in Gut Microbiome Composition between Persons with Chronic Schizophrenia and Healthy Comparison Subjects," *Schizophrenia Research*, September 2018. https://doi.org/10.1016/j.schres.2018.09.014.

Nisbett, Richard E., and Dov Cohen. *Culture of Honor: The Psychology of Violence in the South*. New Directions in Social Psychology. Boulder, Colo: Westview Press, 1996.

Offerman, Theo. "Hurting Hurts More than Helping Helps," *European Economic Review* 46, no. 8 (September 2002): 1423–37. https://doi.org/10.1016/S0014-2921(01)00176-3.

Okun, ArthurM. *Prices and Quantities: A Macroeconomic Analysis*. Washington, D.C: Brookings Institution, 1981.

Ostrom, Elinor. "A Behavioral Approach to the Rational Choice Theory of Collective Action: Presidential Address, American Political Science Association, 1997," *American Political Science Review* 92, no. 01 (March 1998): 1–22. https://doi.org/10.2307/2585925.

Padoa-Schioppa, Camillo, and John A. Assad. "Neurons in the Orbitofrontal Cortex Encode Economic Value," *Nature* 441, no. 7090 (May 2006): 223–26. https://doi.org/10.1038/nature04676.

Pagel, Mark D. *Wired for Culture: Origins of the Human Social Mind*. 1st ed. New York: W.W. Norton, 2013.

Panksepp, Jaak. *Affective Neuroscience: The Foundations of Human and Animal Emotions*. New York, NY, US: Oxford University Press, 1998.

Pavlou, Paul A., and David Gefen. "Building Effective Online Marketplaces with Institution-Based Trust," *Information Systems Research* 15, no. 1 (March 2004): 37–59. https://doi.org/10.1287/isre.1040.0015.

Phan, K. L., C. S. Sripada, M. Angstadt, and K. McCabe. "Reputation for Reciprocity Engages the Brain Reward Center," *Proceedings of the National Academy of Sciences* 107, no. 29 (July 20, 2010): 13099–104. https://doi.org/10.1073/pnas.1008137107.

Pink, Daniel H. *Drive: The Surprising Truth about What Motivates Us*. First paperback edition. New York]: Riverhead Books, 2011.

Pinker, Steven. *The Blank Slate: The Modern Denial of Human Nature*. New York: Viking, 2002.

Plassmann, H., J. O'Doherty, and A. Rangel. "Orbitofrontal Cortex Encodes Willingness to Pay in Everyday Economic Transactions," *Journal of Neuroscience* 27, no. 37 (September 12, 2007): 9984–88. https://doi.org/10.1523/JNEUROSCI.2131-07.2007.

Polanyi, Karl. *The Great Transformation: The Political and Economic Origins of Our Time*. 2nd Beacon Paperback ed. Boston, MA: Beacon Press, 2001.

Polezzi, D, I Daum, E Rubaltelli, L Lotto, C Civai, G Sartori, and R Rumiati. "Mentalizing in Economic Decision-Making," *Behavioural Brain Research* 190, no. 2 (July 19, 2008): 218–23. https://doi.org/10.1016/j.bbr.2008.03.003.

Rand, David G., and Martin A. Nowak. "The Evolution of Antisocial Punishment in Optional Public Goods Games," *Nature Communications* 2, no. 1 (September 2011). https://doi.org/10.1038/ncomms1442.

Richardson, Brendan. *Tribal Marketing, Tribal Branding*. London: Palgrave Macmillan UK, 2013. https://doi.org/10.1057/9781137349101.

Richerson, Peter J., and Robert Boyd. Not by Genes Alone: How Culture Transformed Human Evolution. *Not by Genes Alone: How Culture Transformed Human Evolution*. Chicago, IL, US: University of Chicago Press, 2005.

Rilling, James K., David A. Gutman, Thorsten R. Zeh, Giuseppe Pagnoni, Gregory S. Berns, and Clinton D. Kilts. "A Neural Basis for Social Cooperation," *Neuron* 35, no. 2 (July 2002): 395–405. https://doi.org/10.1016/S0896-6273(02)00755-9.

Rilling, James K, Brooks King-Casas, and Alan G Sanfey. "The Neurobiology of Social Decision-Making," *Current Opinion in Neurobiology* 18, no. 2 (April 2008): 159–65. https://doi.org/10.1016/j.conb.2008.06.003.

Rizzolatti, Giacomo, and Laila Craighero. "The Mirror-Neuron System," *Annual Review of Neuroscience* 27, no. 1 (July 21, 2004): 169–92. https://doi.org/10.1146/annurev.neuro.27.070203.144230.

Robert Axelrod, and William D. Hamilton. "The Evolution of Cooperation," *Science, New Series* 211, no. 4489 (1981): 1390–96.

Robson, Arthur J. "Evolution and Human Nature," *Journal of Economic Perspectives* 16, no. 2 (May 2002): 89–106. https://doi.org/10.1257/0895330027274.

Russell, James A. "Core Affect and the Psychological Construction of Emotion," *Psychological Review* 110, no. 1 (January 2003): 145–72.

Sahlins, Marshall. *Stone Age Economics*. London; New York, NY: Routledge Classics, 2017.

Schino, Gabriele, and Filippo Aureli. "Chapter 2 Reciprocal Altruism in Primates," In *Advances in the Study of Behavior*, 39:45–69. Elsevier, 2009. https://doi.org/10.1016/S0065-3454(09)39002-6.

Schwartz, Lisa M., and Steven Woloshin. "Medical Marketing in the United States, 1997-2016," *JAMA* 321, no. 1 (January 1, 2019): 80. https://doi.org/10.1001/jama.2018.19320.

Seabright, Paul. *The Company of Strangers: A Natural History of Economic Life*. Princeton, N.J.: Princeton University Press, 2010. http://public.eblib.com/choice/publicfullrecord.aspx?p=557159.

———. "The Three Musketeers: What Do We Still Need to Know About Our Passage Through Prehistory?" *Biological Theory* 6, no. 2 (June 2011): 127–31. https://doi.org/10.1007/s13752-012-0017-7.

Selenko, Eva, Anne Mäkikangas, and Christopher B. Stride. "Does Job Insecurity Threaten Who You Are? Introducing a Social Identity Perspective to Explain Well-Being and Performance Consequences of Job Insecurity: Social Identity Perspective on Job Insecurity," *Journal of Organizational Behavior* 38, no. 6 (July 2017): 856–75. https://doi.org/10.1002/job.2172.

Sescousse, G., J. Redouté, and J.-C. Dreher. "The Architecture of Reward Value Coding in the Human Orbitofrontal Cortex," *Journal of Neuroscience* 30, no. 39 (September 29, 2010): 13095–104. https://doi.org/10.1523/JNEUROSCI.3501-10.2010.

Sgritta, Martina, Sean W. Dooling, Shelly A. Buffington, Eric N. Momin, Michael B. Francis, Robert A. Britton, and Mauro Costa-Mattioli. "Mechanisms Underlying Microbial-Mediated Changes in Social Behavior in Mouse Models of Autism Spectrum Disorder," *Neuron* 101, no. 2 (January 2019): 246–259.e6. https://doi.org/10.1016/j.neuron.2018.11.018.

Shackle, G. L. S. *Epistemics & Economics: A Critique of Economic Doctrines*. Cambridge [Eng.]: University Press, 1972.

Shackelford, T. K., and D.M. Buss. Betrayal in mateships, friendships, and coalitions. *Personality and Social Psychology Bulletin* 22, no. 11 (1996): 1151–64. http://dx.doi.org/10.1177/01461672962211006

Shestakova, Anna, Jörg Rieskamp, Sergey Tugin, Alexey Ossadtchi, Janina Krutitskaya, and Vasily Klucharev. "Electrophysiological Precursors of Social Conformity," *Social Cognitive and Affective Neuroscience* 8, no. 7 (October 1, 2013): 756–63. https://doi.org/10.1093/scan/nss064.

Shubin, Neil. *Your Inner Fish: A Journey into the 3.5-Billion-Year History of the Human Body*. 1st Vintage Books ed. New York: Vintage Books, 2009.

Silk, Joan B. "Cooperation without Counting: The Puzzle of Friendship," In *Genetic and Cultural Evolution of Cooperation*, (2003): 37–54.

Simion, Francesca, Elisa Di Giorgio, Irene Leo, and Lara Bardi. "The Processing of Social Stimuli in Early Infancy," In *Progress in Brain Research*, 189:173–93. Elsevier, 2011. https://doi.org/10.1016/B978-0-444-53884-0.00024-5.

Simion, Francesca, Viola Macchi Cassia, Chiara Turati, and Eloisa Valenza. "The Origins of Face Perception: Specific versus Non-Specific Mechanisms," *Infant and Child Development* 10, no. 1–2 (March 2001): 59–65. https://doi.org/10.1002/icd.247.

Simon, Herbert. "A Mechanism for Social Selection and Successful Altruism," *Science, New Series* 250, no. 4988 (1990): 1665–68.

Simon, Herbert A. "A Behavioral Model of Rational Choice," *The Quarterly Journal of Economics* 69, no. 1 (February 1955): 99. https://doi.org/10.2307/1884852.

Simon, Herbert A. "Organizations and Markets," *Journal of Economic Perspectives* 5, no. 2 (May 1991): 25–44. https://doi.org/10.1257/jep.5.2.25.

Simon, Herbert Alexander. *Reason in Human Affairs*. Stanford, Calif: Stanford Univ. Press, 1983.

Singer, Tania, Ben Seymour, John O'Doherty, Holger Kaube, Raymond J. Dolan, and Chris D. Frith. "Empathy for Pain Involves the Affective but Not Sensory Components of Pain." *Science* 303, no. 5661 (February 20, 2004): 1157. https://doi.org/10.1126/science.1093535.

Singer, Tania, and Ernst Fehr. "The Neuroeconomics of Mind Reading and Empathy," *American Economic Review* 95, no. 2 (April 2005): 340–45. https://doi.org/10.1257/000282805774670103.

Sivanathan, Niro, and Nathan C. Pettit. "Protecting the Self through Consumption: Status Goods as Affirmational Commodities," *Journal of Experimental Social Psychology* 46, no. 3 (May 2010): 564–70. https://doi.org/10.1016/j.jesp.2010.01.006.

Skarlicki, Daniel P, and Robert Folger. "Retaliation in the Workplace: The Roles of Distributive, Procedural, and Interactional Justice," *Journal of Applied Psychology* 82, no. 3 (June 1997): 434–43. http://dx.doi.org/10.1037/0021-9010.82.3.434.

Slovic, Paul, Melissa L. Finucane, Ellen Peters, and Donald G. MacGregor. "The Affect Heuristic," *European Journal of Operational Research* 177, no. 3 (March 2007): 1333–52. https://doi.org/10.1016/j.ejor.2005.04.006.

Smith, Adam. "Cognitive Empathy and Emotional Empathy in Human Behavior and Evolution," *The Psychological Record* 56, no. 1 (January 2006): 3–21. https://doi.org/10.1007/BF03395534.

Smith, Adam. *The Wealth of Nations*. Bantam classic ed. New York, N.Y: Bantam Classic, 2003.

Smith, Vernon L. "Constructivist and Ecological Rationality in Economics," *The American Economic Review* 93, no. 3 (2003): 465–508.

———. *Rationality in Economics: Constructivist and Ecological Forms*. Cambridge; New York: Cambridge University Press, 2008.

Sperber, Dan. "Anthropology and Psychology: Towards an Epidemiology of Representations," *Man* 20, no. 1 (March 1985): 73. https://doi.org/10.2307/2802222.

Stallen, Mirre, and Alan G. Sanfey. "The Neuroscience of Social Conformity: Implications for Fundamental and Applied Research," *Frontiers in Neuroscience* 9 (September 28, 2015). https://doi.org/10.3389/fnins.2015.00337.

Stewart, Jack. "Don't Freak Over Boeing's Self-Flying Plane—Robots Already Run the Skies," *Wired*, June 9, 2017. https://www.wired.com/story/boeing-autonomous-plane-autopilot/.

Strang, Sabrina, Xenia Grote, Katarina Kuss, Soyoung Q. Park, and Bernd Weber. "Generalized Negative Reciprocity in the Dictator Game—How to Interrupt the Chain of Unfairness," *Scientific Reports* 6, no. 1 (April 2016). https://doi.org/10.1038/srep22316.

Takahashi, H., M. Matsuura, M. Koeda, N. Yahata, T. Suhara, M. Kato, and Y. Okubo. "Brain Activations during Judgments of Positive Self-Conscious Emotion and Positive Basic Emotion: Pride and Joy," *Cerebral Cortex* 18, no. 4 (April 1, 2008): 898–903. https://doi.org/10.1093/cercor/bhm120.

Thaler, Richard H., and Cass R. Sunstein. *Nudge: Improving Decisions about Health, Wealth, and Happiness*. Rev. and expanded ed. New York: Penguin Books, 2009.

Thompson, J. C., M. Clarke, T. Stewart, A. Puce. "Configural Processing of Biological Motion in Human Superior Temporal Sulcus," *Journal of Neuroscience* 25, no. 39 (September 28, 2005): 9059–66. https://doi.org/10.1523/JNEUROSCI.2129-05.2005.

Todorov, A., A.N. Mandisodza, A. Goren, C.C. Hall. "Inferences of Competence from Faces Predict Election Outcomes," *Science* 308, no. 5728 (June 10, 2005): 1623–26. https://doi.org/10.1126/science.1110589.

Tomasello, Michael. "Opinion | For Human Eyes Only," *The New York Times*, January 13, 2007, sec. Opinion. https://www.nytimes.com/2007/01/13/opinion/13tomasello.html.

Tomasello, Michael, and Malinda Carpenter. "Shared Intentionality," *Developmental Science* 10, no. 1 (January 2007): 121–25. https://doi.org/10.1111/j.1467-7687.2007.00573.x.

Tooby, John, and Leda Cosmides. "Conceptual Foundations of Evolutionary Psychology," In *The Handbook of Evolutionary Psychology*, edited by David M. Buss, 5–67. Hoboken, NJ, USA: John Wiley & Sons, Inc., 2015. https://doi.org/10.1002/9780470939376.ch1.

Trivers, Robert L. "The Evolution of Reciprocal Altruism," *The Quarterly Review of Biology* 46, no. 1 (1971): 35–57.

Tuomela, Raimo. *The Philosophy of Sociality: The Shared Point of View*. Oxford [England]; New York: Oxford University Press, 2007.

Ubel, Peter A. *Free Market Madness: Why Human Nature Is at Odds with Economics--and Why It Matters*. Boston, Mass: Harvard Business Press, 2009.

Van Overwalle, Frank. "A Dissociation between Social Mentalizing and General Reasoning," *NeuroImage* 54, no. 2 (January 2011): 1589–99. https://doi.org/10.1016/j.neuroimage.2010.09.043.

Veblen, T. *The Theory of the Leisure Class: An Economic Study of Institutions. Macmillan Standard Library*. Macmillan, 1912. https://books.google.com/books?id=hdc3AAAAMAAJ.

Vignemont, Frederique de, and Tania Singer. "The Empathic Brain: How, When and Why?" *Trends in Cognitive Sciences* 10, no. 10 (October 2006): 435–41. https://doi.org/10.1016/j.tics.2006.08.008.

Vlaev, Ivo, Nick Chater, Neil Stewart, and Gordon D.A. Brown. "Does the Brain Calculate Value?" *Trends in Cognitive Sciences* 15, no. 11 (November 2011): 546–54. https://doi.org/10.1016/j.tics.2011.09.008.

Vohs, Kathleen D., Nicole L. Mead, and Miranda R. Goode. "The Psychological Consequences of Money," *Science* 314, no. 5802 (November 17, 2006): 1154. https://doi.org/10.1126/science.1132491.

Waal, Frans B. M. de. *Our Inner Ape: A Leading Primatologist Explains Why We Are Who We Are*. Science/Nature. New York: Riverhead Books, 2006.

Waal, Frans B.M. de. "Food Sharing and Reciprocal Obligations among Chimpanzees," *Journal of Human Evolution* 18, no. 5 (August 1989): 433–59. https://doi.org/10.1016/0047-2484(89)90074-2.

Walter, Henrik, Birgit Abler, Angela Ciaramidaro, and Susanne Erk. "Motivating Forces of Human Actions," *Brain Research Bulletin* 67, no. 5 (November 2005): 368–81. https://doi.org/10.1016/j.brainresbull.2005.06.016.

Walter, Henrik, Mauro Adenzato, Angela Ciaramidaro, Ivan Enrici, Lorenzo Pia, and Bruno G. Bara. "Understanding Intentions in Social Interaction: The Role of the Anterior Paracingulate Cortex," *Journal of Cognitive Neuroscience* 16, no. 10 (December 2004): 1854–63. https://doi.org/10.1162/0898929042947838.

Wardle, Jane, and Lucy Cooke. "Genetic and Environmental Determinants of Children's Food Preferences," *British Journal of Nutrition* 99, no. S1 (February 2008). https://doi.org/10.1017/S000711450889246X.

Wason, P. C. "Reasoning about a Rule," *Quarterly Journal of Experimental Psychology* 20, no. 3 (August 1968): 273–81. https://doi.org/10.1080/14640746808400161.

Watt, Douglas F. "Reflections on the Neuroscientific Legacy of Jaak Panksepp (1943–2017)," *Neuropsychoanalysis* 19, no. 2 (July 3, 2017): 183–98. https://doi.org/10.1080/15294145.2017.1376549.

Wettlaufer, Jörg. "Neurohistorical and Evolutionary Aspects of a History of Shame and Shaming." In *Environment, Culture, and the Brain: New Explorations in Neurohistory*, edited by Edmund Russell, RCC Perspectives 2012, no. 6, 49–53. doi.org/10.5282/rcc/5596

Whiten, Andrew, and Erica van de Waal. "Social Learning, Culture and the 'Socio-Cultural Brain' of Human and Non-Human Primates," *Neuroscience & Biobehavioral Reviews* 82 (November 2017): 58–75. https://doi.org/10.1016/j.neubiorev.2016.12.018.

Williams, Steve, Richard Pitre, and Mohamed Zainuba. "Justice and Organizational Citizenship Behavior Intentions: Fair Rewards Versus Fair Treatment," *The Journal of Social Psychology* 142, no. 1 (February 2002): 33–44. https://doi.org/10.1080/00224540209603883.

Williamson, Oliver E. *Markets and Hierarchies: Analysis and Antitrust Implications: A Study in the Economics of Internal Organization*. Free Press, 1975.

Wilson, Daniel R. "The Evolutionary Neuroscience of Human Reciprocal Sociality: A Basic Outline for Economists," *The Journal of Socio-Economics* 35, no. 4 (August 2006): 626–33. https://doi.org/10.1016/j.socec.2005.12.020.

Xiang, T., T. Lohrenz, and P. R. Montague. "Computational Substrates of Norms and Their Violations during Social Exchange," *Journal of Neuroscience* 33, no. 3 (January 16, 2013): 1099–1108. https://doi.org/10.1523/JNEUROSCI.1642-12.2013.

Xiao, E., and D. Houser. "Emotion Expression in Human Punishment Behavior," *Proceedings of the National Academy of Sciences* 102, no. 20 (May 17, 2005): 7398–7401. https://doi.org/10.1073/pnas.0502399102.

Zeelenberg, M, and R Pieters. "A Theory of Regret Regulation 1.0," *Journal of Consumer Psychology* 17, no. 1 (January 2007): 3–18. https://doi.org/10.1207/s15327663jcp1701_3.

Zeelenberg, Marcel, and Rik Pieters. "Feeling Is for Doing: A Pragmatic Approach to the Study of Emotions in Economic Behavior," In *Social Psychology and Economics*, 117–37. Mahwah, NJ, US: Lawrence Erlbaum Associates Publishers, 2006.

Index

www.ingramcontent.com/pod-product-compliance
Lightning Source LLC
LaVergne TN
LVHW021112300926
849160LV00009B/699